AN ADAPTED CLAS

Beowulf

GLOBE FEARON EDUCATIONAL PUBLISHER
Upper Saddle River, New Jersey
www.globefearon.com

Adapter: Sandra Widener
Project Editor: Wendy R. Diskin
Senior Editor: Lynn Kloss
Production Editor: Travis Bailey
Marketing Manager: Gloria Sammur
Art Supervision: Sharon Ferguson
Electronic Page Production: Jennifer Pereira
Cover and Interior Illustrator: Karen Locisano

Printed in the United States of America
1 2 3 4 5 6 7 8 9 10 03 02 01 00 99

ISBN 0-835-95541-9

GLOBE FEARON EDUCATIONAL PUBLISHER
Upper Saddle River, New Jersey
www.globefearon.com

CONTENTS

THE ORIGINS OF BEOWULF

Beowulf is one of the oldest poems written in the English language. It has been studied and examined for centuries.

Beowulf was written in Old English, which sounds like a foreign language to today's English speakers. It is the longest surviving poem in Old English. When *Beowulf* was written is a matter of debate—estimates range from the eighth century A.D. to the tenth century A.D. Scholars have tried to decide when it was written based on how the author used Old English words and grammar. *Beowulf* was written about events that were supposed to have themselves happened two hundred years before the poem was written.

Beowulf's author is a mystery. Some scholars guess that the author was a court poet, one who wrote poetry sung to the music of a harp. Others believe the poet was a monk. Most agree that the person who wrote *Beowulf* had training in writing poetry. The poem was written to be recited before a group of people, not read silently, as most poetry is read today.

A tale such as *Beowulf* would likely have been composed for several reasons. One reason may be that it served to entertain listeners, especially the king and his court. There are many references within the poem to royal families, bits of history, and battles. These references served to pass down the heritage and history of a people. Storytellers and poets were considered the keepers of history.

For centuries, the poem had been kept in a monastery in England. Then King Henry VIII closed most of the monasteries during his reign from 1509 to 1547. During these years, many of the books in the monasteries were sent across the English Channel to Europe, where the pages were used for wrapping meat at butchers' shops. At least one scholar, Lawrence Nowell, realized what was being lost. He saved *Beowulf*, among other books.

The manuscript next passed to Sir Robert Cotton. He cataloged it along with many other ancient manuscripts. From 1642 to 1646 a civil war in England threatened *Beowulf* again. Puritans were burning books. Sheriff Bromfall of Blunham came to the rescue this time, storing books from Cotton's collection in another town.

The next threat was fire. In 1731, the Cotton collection was being stored in a house when a fire burned many of the books and scorched others. *Beowulf* was burned around the edges. The manuscript's burnt edges began to crumble. Before the fire, however, a Danish scholar had made a copy of the original. That copy was later used to reconstruct the unreadable, charred parts of the original.

Since 1733, the original copy of the poem has been at the British Museum in London. The curators there have carefully placed each page in clear plastic for protection. There are some places where lines or words are missing, but scholars can still read the poem.

ADAPTER'S NOTE

In preparing this edition of *Beowulf*, we have kept as close as possible to the style and meaning of the original. We have changed some of the vocabulary. We have also shortened some passages. Some of the footnotes explain difficult words. Other footnotes fill in historical details of the story. As is typical of most translations people read today, the poem is now written in narrative form.

PREFACE

Beowulf is noteworthy as an example of early poetry, but even more, it is a tale of stirring adventure. This poem tells of some of the universal themes of humankind—good and evil, loyalty, courage. As we read the poem, we are introduced to the royal families of the Geats and the Danes. Then, in what are essentially three sections, we read about the exploits of Beowulf, a Geat prince. Beowulf, who is a heroic figure of larger-than-life proportions, travels across the sea in the first section to fight the monster Grendel. Grendel has been terrorizing the Danish king Hrothgar's castle for more than a decade. In the second section, Beowulf fights Grendel's mother in a battle that occurs deep under a bloody lake. In the last section, which occurs 50 years later, Beowulf is an old king who battles one last time with a fire-breathing dragon. In *Beowulf,* the great themes the poet tackles are illustrated with a story that continues to compel readers today, more than a thousand years after it was written.

HISTORICAL BACKGROUND

The story of *Beowulf* takes place in the fifth or sixth century A.D. It is set in northern Europe. The Danes' country is what is now Denmark and the southern tip of today's Sweden. The Swedes lived in northern Sweden. Trying to pinpoint the Geats' homeland is more difficult. In this poem, the Geats live in what is now southern Sweden, an area of land located between the Danes and the Swedes.

There is evidence that some of the characters in *Beowulf* actually existed. A monk who wrote a history of the Franks tells of a king named Hygelac who raided the Franks' territory along the Rhine in 520. That event is mentioned in the poem. Beowulf, however, appears to be a fictional character.

In 1939, a seventh-century burial ship was discovered in an estuary of the River Deben in Suffolk, England. The discovery helped add more details to what we know about the time during which *Beowulf* was set. It was a burial ship like that in which Scyld Scefing is sent off at the beginning of *Beowulf*. The ship was filled with treasures that showed a high level of both wealth and art. By studying the items from that ship we can imagine the scene in the great castle of Heorot. The walls would be hung with tapestries spun with gold. The hall would be filled with finely carved benches and long tables. During mealtimes, the tables would be set for the warriors' meals. At night, the tables would be made into beds for the same warriors. At one end of the hall the carved and gilded throne for the king would rise higher than the other furniture. The king's table would be set with glassware and cups encrusted with jewels, and the royal party would be dressed in finely made fabrics and would be wearing golden jewelry.

Finding the burial ship also gave scholars more insight into the question of religion during the time the events in *Beowulf* occurred. There were both Christian items and pagan items in the ship. Paganism, the religion in place before Christianity, was based on a belief in many gods and natural forces. When the poem was written, pagan beliefs were being replaced by Christian beliefs. The poem shows this transition.

The monsters in *Beowulf*, for example, are descendants of Cain. Cain is a figure from Judeo-Christian history. He killed his brother Abel and was an outcast from God because of this. The poem mentions the will of God often, which reflects the poet's belief that God determined the daily events and fate of humans. This belief is similar to the pagan idea of fate determining events. Another pagan custom shown in *Beowulf* is the funeral ship and the funeral pyre. Both were intended to help the passage of a dead person into the next world. When Christianity became widespread, those funeral practices were banned.

The structure of society during the days of *Beowulf* explains the motivation of many of the actions of the characters. Warriors pledged loyalty to a king, and they pledged to defend that king whenever necessary. In return, the warriors received a share of the king's wealth and the king's protection. The worst fate a warrior could face was to be exiled by his king. If that happened, the warrior was on his own, outside society, and with no way of making a living.

The pledge of loyalty meant that the wrongful death of a king must be avenged by his warriors. Warriors were also expected to avenge the murder of relatives. They did this by killing a member of the family that had killed their relative. In this time, the idea of blood money became an alternative to this bloodshed. If you killed a person and paid money to his family, the feud would be forgotten. There are several instances of this practice in *Beowulf.* In the section where the fight of the Finns is related, vengeance for kings' deaths fuels a terrible feud between peoples. The story of the accidental death of one prince caused by another is a second example. The father, King Hrethel, faces a terrible dilemma. He would have to kill one son to avenge the death of the other. The conflict leads to King Hrethel's death from grief.

The time during which *Beowulf* occurred was in many ways the transition between the old and the new. Blood vengeance was being replaced by blood money. Paganism was being replaced by Christianity. Even so, it was a world where physical power and bravery were linked to success, and where society was governed by bands of warriors fiercely loyal to their king.

MAJOR CHARACTERS OF *BEOWULF*

Beowulf includes dozens of characters—Danes, Geats, Swedes, monsters. Here are some of the most important.

THE DANES

Aeschere favorite warrior and best friend of King Hrothgar

Beow not the Beowulf of the poem; son of Scyld

Healfdene son of Beow, king himself, and father of Hrothgar, Heorogar, and Halga

Heremod ancient king who serves as an example of how not to rule

Hrothgar king when Beowulf fights Grendel; son of Healfdene and brother of Heorogar and Halga

Scyld Scefing king who begins a famous line of kings

Unferth killed his brother; early on, is jealous of Beowulf's fame, but comes to accept Beowulf's superiority

Wealhtheow Hrothgar's queen

THE GEATS

Beowulf hero of the poem, nephew of Hygelac, later king of the Geats

Ecgtheow father of Beowulf, King Hrethel's son-in-law, kills a man, seeks shelter in Denmark with Hrothgar

Haethcyn son of King Hrethel, he accidentally kills his brother Herebeald while they are hunting

Heardred King of the Geats, he is aided by Beowulf and killed by the Swedish king Onela

Herebeald brother of Haethcyn and Hygelac; killed by his brother Haethcyn in a hunting accident

Hrethel king who dies of grief after his son Herebeald is killed in a hunting accident by his brother

Hygd Queen of Hygelac, and mother of Heardred

Hygelac Geatish king and uncle to Beowulf

Wiglaf helps Beowulf in his fight against the dragon and becomes king of the Geats

THE SWEDES

Eadgils Swedish prince; King Onela's nephew; brother of Eanmund

Eanmund Eadgils's brother

Onela Swedish king killed by Beowulf and Eadgils after Onela kills the Geatish king Heardred

CHARACTERS FROM THE STORY OF THE FINNS

Finn King of the Frisians; killed by the Danes

Hengest Hnaef's brother and then king of the Danes

Hildeburh Finn's wife and Danish king Hnaef's sister

Hnaef Danish king, brother of Hengest and Hildeburh, killed by Finn

MONSTERS

Grendel descendant of Cain, Grendel is a huge, misshapen monster

Grendel's mother descendant of Cain and a monster herself

Dragon guard of a treasure left by a now-vanished people

Sea monsters found both in the sea and in the lake where Grendel and his mother live

TRIBES

Danes ruled by Scyld Scefing, Beow, Healfdene, Hrothgar, and finally Hrothulf

Geats from southern Sweden; ruled by Hrethel, Haethcyn, Hygelac, Heardred, and finally Beowulf

Franks from what is now France; they are Germanic people who join the Frisians to defeat Hygelac

Frisians western Germanic people living in what is now Holland; ruled by King Finn, Hnaef, and finally Hengest

Swedes ruled by Ongentheow, Onela, and then Eadgils

Prologue:
The Early History of the Danes

Listen to my story! We have heard of the long-ago years, of the glory of the Danish kings. We have heard how they swung their mighty swords in brave deeds.

In those days Scyld Scefing made slaves of enemy soldiers and terrified their nobles. The Danes had found him helpless as a child. He had been floating on the sea in a ship, surrounded by gifts, a strange kingchild. He grew tall, sailed the seas, rode through the land, till other kings sailed the whale-paths[1] to seek him, offer him gold, and bow to him. He ruled lands on all sides. That was a brave king!

Time brought to him, to his people, a son. He was a gift for the Danes. Before Scyld's coming they had lived kingless and miserable. Scyld's son Beow became famous, the glory of the Danes. While still in his father's house he made himself beloved by the warriors. So should a prince show his strength, by his father's side, forging warriors into friends. Later in Beow's life these warriors would stand with him.

When his hour had come, Scyld the brave died, still strong but called to the Lord. His warriors took their dear friend back to the sea, as he had asked. Ready on the shore stood a proud ship, a king's ship. They laid down their beloved king there.

Never was there a grave ship with more gold and riches. They heaped up treasures, coats of armor, jeweled helmets, swords. On his breast were heaps of jewels. He had as many gifts with him in death as he had when he had first sailed across the sea as a child. They set a golden banner far above his head and let

---

1. **whale-paths** seas

the water take him. Their spirits were sad, their minds mournful. No one knows where that ship with its silent cargo of gold and king finally landed.

Chapter 1

Then Beow became king of the Danes, a beloved king, known among the nations of the world as a brave leader, a king to respect. In his turn, he gave his people a son, the great Healfdene. To the end of his long life, Beow ruled the Danes well, wise and fierce in battle.

To Healfdene were born four children, Heorogar and Hrothgar and Halga the Good, and one daughter, Yrs. She became the wife of Onela, king of the Swedes, and was their queen.

Then Hrothgar took the throne of the Danes, and he became king. To Hrothgar was given success in battle, glory in war. Warriors were glad to follow him, and his armies swelled with eager young men.

Hrothgar thought of greatness, and he resolved to build a hall, a castle larger than men had ever seen, a mead-hall[2] for all his warriors. Hrothgar wanted to share what he had gained. In this mead-hall he promised to divide the spoils of their victories and give to his warriors what they had earned.

Workers came from over the earth to help build that most beautiful of castles. Quickly it was finished, towering above all others. Hrothgar gave the dwelling the name Heorot, which means *deer*. Hrothgar kept

---

2. **mead**   a beerlike drink; the mead-hall was similar
   to a castle

his promise, and there was a banquet where he handed out rings and treasure to his warriors.

An evil demon, who dwelt in the darkness, listened in pain to every word spoken in the castle. Every day there was the sound of the harp, the clear voice of the poet singing of how the Almighty made the earth, shaped the oceans and the plains, set the moon and the sun. The demon listened as the warriors laughed joyfully in the hall.

This cold wanderer, the monster living down in the darkness, stirred. He was enraged by the joy of the warriors. This grim beast was called Grendel, and he roamed the moors,[3] his home a hell on earth. The monster was born of the descendants of Cain, he who had murdered his brother Abel and was punished forever by God for the death. God drove Cain out, shutting him away from people. Cain's descendants became a tribe of evil—fiends, demons, monsters, goblins, giants. They were forever doomed, forever opposing the Lord, again and again scorned.

Chapter 2

The night of the celebration the monster Grendel came to the castle to see where the warriors had gone after the feast. He found them sprawled in sleep, dreaming happily, suspecting nothing. The monster's rage was as quick as his claws. He snatched up 30 of the sleeping warriors and slaughtered them. Grendel carried the bloody bodies back to his lair, delighted with the night's grim work.

---

3. moors marshland, swamps

Grendel's deeds were known with the first light of dawn. The warriors in the castle ended their long feast with a great cry and weeping. Their good king Hrothgar, the hero of earlier days, sat stunned in grief, suffering from the death of his warriors. From the tracks left behind, Hrothgar could see that a terrible monster had torn his warriors apart.

That night, Grendel came again; the thirst for murder was upon him. He slaughtered still more warriors, rejoicing in his terrible deeds. After that night, most of the warriors tried to escape, to find other beds far from the castle. It was clear to them that Grendel now controlled the hall, and that he hated them with a deep passion.

So Grendel ruled the castle, one against many. The castle Heorot stood empty and deserted. Hrothgar, the brave king, mourned for 12 cold winters. Throughout Denmark and across the seas, the songs were told of Grendel, Heorot's monster. The songs told of Grendel's rage, how Grendel fought against Hrothgar, his crimes unending. Grendel wanted no peace. He did not want to settle this war. Grendel's only answer to killing one warrior was to kill another.

Grendel waited in the darkness, stalking Hrothgar's men, a dark death shadow ambushing and devouring warriors young and old. He was always there at the edge of the marsh, waiting, unseen.

The monster killed when he could, living his dark nights in the castle, Heorot. Yet he could not touch Hrothgar's throne, which was protected by God.

Hrothgar spent his days in despair. His spirit was broken. The wise men of Hrothgar's castle would sit in council talking of the terror. The wise men considered plans, thought of what might be done. But what could even the bravest of warriors do against this monster? At times, in desperation, they offered sacrifices, praying that the devil himself might aid them. They were heathens[4] and knew no better. Their ears did not know the Lord's praise, nor did they know His glory. Woe to the man who in terrible trouble seeks the devil. Hail to those who rise to God and seek out his peace.

Chapter 3

Hrothgar brooded over his troubles. Too harsh was the fate that had come upon the king and his people. The cruelty, the evil, and the violence hung over them all.

Far away in the land of the Geats, Beowulf, King Hygelac's warrior, heard the tales of Grendel's deeds. Beowulf was the strongest of the Geats, the strongest of all men living then. Beowulf ordered a ship be made ready and announced he would sail across the seas to help Hrothgar.

Beowulf was much loved among the Geats, but Hrothgar needed his help, so the wise men urged the adventure on. The wise men checked the omens, which were good. From the bravest men of the kingdom, Beowulf chose 14 to go with him.

They marched down to the ship, stored their gleaming weapons. Then the men shoved off from shore, anxious to be on their way. Beowulf knew the sea. He pointed the ship straight to the far away Danish shore. The ship traveled over the sea waves like a bird, until on the second day they came to

---

4. **heathens** those who belong to a tribe or nation that does not acknowledge the God of Judaism, Christianity, or Islam

where they could see the sea cliffs of land. The wind went out of the sails, and they quietly ended their voyage. Quickly the Geat warriors climbed over the side, their chain mail[5] clanking, and went down the gangplank to shore.

From his post high on land, a Danish watcher, whose job it was to guard the sea cliffs, saw the travelers headed to shore. He saw their shining shields and spurred his horse to ride to the warriors and learn who they were.

Shaking his heavy spear, the warrior of Hrothgar demanded, "Who are you, dressed in armor ready for battle? Why do you come sailing over the seas to this land? I have long watched this coast for the king so none of our enemies may enter Denmark. I do not remember an army landing so openly. I know of no permission for your landing here.

"Never have I seen a mightier man than your leader. He has noble bearing, and no man carries such weapons unless he is royal. I must know who you are now, right away. Tell me your name, and your father's! None wishing the Danes harm can go farther onto Danish soil than you have already. Tell me now, quickly! Speak exactly who you are, and why you have come."

Chapter 4

Beowulf answered the Danish watcher. "We are Geats, men who follow Hygelac. My father was a noble leader named Ecgtheow. He lived to be an old man—wise men all over the earth still remember

---

5. **chain mail** or **mail shirts**   armor made of linked rings of chain

him. We have come with only good intentions to your land. We seek your king, Hrothgar, the son of Healfdene, on a great mission. Advise us well and help us to seek him!

"Our business is not secret; it is not hidden or dark. You have heard of the monster that curses your country, a strange, mysterious fiend that travels in the dark night in hatred. We have heard the monster brings great slaughter.

"I hope to offer advice and help your wise ruler Hrothgar find an end to these sorrows. Unless the monster is broken, the time of darkness and bloodgrief will continue in this land."

The watchman answered Beowulf boldly. "A warrior with keen wits who thinks carefully knows the difference between words and deeds. I believe you, and I trust in your friendship. I will lead you myself to the hall above, and tell my fellow warriors to guard your ship until you return with it to the land of the Geats. May God grant that you pass safely through this battle and return to the Geats."

They set off, their shields and war masks flashing in the sun, marching as though ready to fight. They marched until they could see the golden roofs of Heorot. Their guide, the watchman, pointed out the glittering, brilliant castle, and said, "May the Lord protect you. Keeping the coasts safe is my job, and I must return to it."

Chapter 5

The road to the castle was paved with stones. The Geats traveled that road, and arrived at the castle with their coats of mail shining. Wearily, they lay down their shields, set their spears against the wall. This was an army worthy of its weapons.

A Danish noble, Wulfgar, asked who they were. "Where are you from, with these gold-covered shields, your mail shirts and helmets, your battle gear? I am Hrothgar's captain. Strangers have come before, but never so boldly, so proud. My instincts tell me you are welcome callers, and your courage has brought you here."

The noble, Wulfgar, was answered by the Geats' proud prince. "We are Hygelac's companions, his warriors. Beowulf is my name. I will tell my errand to Hrothgar, Healfdene's son, if he is so good as to let me address him."

Wulfgar, a prince famous for both his strength and his wisdom, then said, "I will ask the lord of the Danes, Hrothgar, about this, as you request. I will tell our glorious ruler about your arrival and tell you his answer."

Wulfgar walked quickly to where Hrothgar, old and grey, sat. In the custom of that court Wulfgar stood, waiting to be heard. Then he said, "Strangers have come from far away, from the Geatish country, led by a mighty warrior named Beowulf who is powerful and wise. The warriors say, my lord, that they have brought a message for you. They appear worthy, my lord."

Chapter 6

Hrothgar, the king of the Danes, replied: "Why, I know this Beowulf, knew him when he was but a boy. His father was Ecgtheow. Now his brave son has come. From seamen who have been to the Geatish lands I have heard that Beowulf has the strength of 30 in the grip of his hand. Holy God has sent him to us to help us defeat Grendel and end that terror. I shall greet him with treasures for his courage in coming here. Order Beowulf and his warriors to come to me! Tell them how welcome we will make them!"

Wulfgar went to the door and told Beowulf and his men, "Our glorious king knows of your noble ancestry and your brave hearts. You are welcome. Go to him as you are, in armor and helmets, but leave here your shields and your spears. Let them wait until after the talk."

Beowulf rose with his warriors gathered about him. Some stayed to guard the weapons. The rest marched into the castle, Beowulf at the front. His mail shirt shining, his helmet gleaming, Beowulf greeted King Hrothgar. "Hail, Hrothgar! Many were the mighty deeds I did in my youth. Now word has come to us of the monster Grendel. We have heard how this noble castle now stands empty and useless at night, light and life both fleeing.

"Our wisest men told me I must seek you, Hrothgar. They said it was my duty to come here. They have looked on when, bloody from my enemies, I came from a fight where I destroyed a family of giants and at night killed water monsters. It was not easy, but I drove trouble from Geatland, drove away our enemies.

"Now I am called to take on Grendel. Grant me this favor! I ask that I settle this matter alone, kill this monster, and drive evil from these halls. I have heard this monster scorns weapons. I shall use no sword, no weapon. My hands alone will fight for me. I will meet this enemy and fight to the death. Whoever loses this battle will face the judgment of God.

"If I fail, Grendel will do as he has, gorging himself with our bodies. If my time comes, there will be no body to bury. Grendel will dine alone and splash his lair red. If battle takes me, send back this mail shirt covering my breast to Hygelac. It is an heirloom.[6] And now, fate will go as it must."

Chapter 7

King Hrothgar spoke: "Out of kindness and past favors you have come, Beowulf. Many years ago, your father Ecgtheow began a terrible feud. He killed a Wylfing warrior. Your father's people were afraid of war and refused to let him stay, so he traveled to the land of the Danes. I was young then, a new king ruling a kingdom rich in gold and jewels, a land rich in heroes. I bought an end to the feud, sent ancient treasures to the Wylfings to end it. Your father swore to keep the peace.

"It is with pain that I tell you the shame and sorrow Grendel has brought to me. You can see how few warriors we have now—Grendel has murdered them. Many times have warriors boasted they would stay the night, sweep away Grendel's horror with

---

6. heirloom a valued possession handed from generation to generation

their swords. Then, in the morning, in the new light, the castle would be drenched with warriors' blood, the floor stained red after the monster's attack. My soldiers would be still fewer, that many fewer loyal friends, after each frenzy. But now, Beowulf, to the table, and a feast in your honor."

Room was made in the hall for the honored guests, mead brought out for the warriors from across the sea. The brave Geats took their seats, took the golden mead cups. The poet sang, and there was the joy of warriors. Geats and Danes celebrated as one, drinking and rejoicing.

Chapter 8

Then Unferth spoke. He was angry that any other man on earth might have greater fame and glory than he did. Unferth said harshly, "Are you the same Beowulf who challenged Breca to a swimming race in the sea? Both of you were boastful, young, and proud. No one could keep you from foolishly risking your lives. You and Breca raced out of the bay, into the open sea, where the ocean boiled with waves. For seven nights you swam, driven by the waves. Breca won the race, overtaking you. He was stronger. The sea cast Breca on the shore near his home, in Norway, where he was ruler. He truly bested you, Beowulf. You have been lucky so far, but your luck may change if you challenge the fierce monster Grendel."

Beowulf replied, "Well, my friend Unferth, you are full of beer and have spoken a good deal about Breca and me. The true story is different. No one can beat me in swimming. When we were boys Breca and I boasted, as boys will boast, that we two would swim out to the open sea and risk our lives. We did as we said we would. We each carried a sword, to fight whales or sea monsters. He could not swim faster than I, and I resolved to stay by his side. I remained by him for five long nights, until the churning ocean drove us apart. The weather was cold, the waves icy, and then a freezing storm broke out, blackening the sky and forcing us apart in the savage swells.

"Sea monsters surfaced around us, stirred by the fierce weather. My mail shirt did me good, protecting me against the sea monsters' attacks. Then a monster seized me and dragged me below, deep on the bottom. He held me there, but I stabbed him with my sword. I killed the sea monster with my own hand. The sea monster floated lifeless in the sea."

Chapter 9

"The monsters attacked again and again. I slashed back with my blade. They had no feast that day. Instead, the next morning, the monsters lay scattered, dying on the beach, the water bloodied from their deep gashes. After that time, sailors could cross that sea path and feel no fear. No monsters would stop them," Beowulf said.

"That morning, a bright beacon of light lit the sky and the water lay still. I could at last see the land, the sea cliffs, the shore. So fate often saves the brave man when his courage holds.

"Whether it was luck or not, I had killed nine sea monsters. I have never heard a story of a harder fight under heaven. I survived that fight and lived, although weary. The gentle waves of the sea bore me back to the land," Beowulf told.

"Breca's feats were not as great, and I've heard no such tales of your deeds, Unferth. What's more, you murdered your brothers—your own brothers, your closest kin! For that, you will suffer in hell, however clever you are.

"Here is a truth, Unferth: If you were a fierce fighter, if you were truly brave, no foe would have dared to ruin the castle Heorot. You would not leave your king in despair. No Grendel, no monster, could have done this if you were half the man, and half the warrior, you claim. But Grendel murders as he likes, without dread or fear. He expects no fight from the Danes. I will show him soon that he should fear the power and might of the Geats. When the sun rises again, Heorot will be free of the monster. His evil will be gone."

After listening to Beowulf, the king Hrothgar was greatly pleased. Hrothgar was sure, now, that Beowulf would kill the monster. Hrothgar believed in Beowulf's courage, and in his bright spirit.

There was laughter and song among the warriors in the castle, the glad words of men, sounds of happiness and hope. Then Wealhtheow, Hrothgar's queen, dressed in gold, came to greet the warriors with cups of wine. The queen gave the first cup, which was filled to the brim, to Hrothgar. Holding it high, she wished him joy in the feast. Happily the king took the cup, drank with pleasure, and blessed the banquet.

Wealhtheow moved from warrior to warrior, offering each a drink from the jeweled cup. Then it was Beowulf's turn to be served. Wealhtheow greeted the man of the Geats, she gave thanks to God for answering her prayers and bringing a man who could help her people. Beowulf took the cup, drank what she poured. He made a speech, eager for combat. "When I left my country, I made up my mind to kill this monster or be killed myself. I shall live in courage, and slay Grendel, or spend my last night in this hall tonight, and welcome my death!"

Wealhtheow was pleased by his words, by his boasts. She walked gracefully to her lord Hrothgar to sit down by him. The feast continued, the warriors rejoicing in song. Then Hrothgar was tired, ready to take his rest. He knew that as soon as the sun set, Grendel would come to the castle. When night had cast its net, and silent black shapes moved in the shadows, that was when the monster would strike. The entire assembly of warriors rose. Then Hrothgar, the old king, spoke to Beowulf.

"Never before, not since I first took the throne, have I allowed any stranger what I have granted you. Make this mead-hall yours tonight. Keep it free from evil. Fight with glory and brave strength. Keep watch against the fierce monster. If you do this, you will sail home with your ship filled with treasure."

Chapter 10

Then Hrothgar, with his warriors, left the castle and went to find his queen, Wealhtheow. Men have learned that God himself set a guard against Grendel and his evil, to watch over the king and his queen. They were believers in God.

The Geatish man, Beowulf, gathered his courage and trusted his own proud strength. He believed he had the favor of God. He stripped off his mail shirt, his helmet, his sword, gave them all to a servant and told him to keep watch over his war gear until morning.

Then, before he took to his bed to rest, Beowulf declared, "I can match strength with Grendel in a fight. I will not kill him by sword, though that would be the easiest way. Grendel, this fiend, has no sword to strike against me. I shall not use the sword in this fight. Let God in his wisdom decide to reward who he thinks is right!"

Then Beowulf lay down to sleep, his cheek on the pillow. Around him his brave warriors did the same and sank to sleep. None of the warriors thought that they would ever return from that faraway place to their native land, to the people they knew and the parents who raised them. Each thought of the Danes already murdered by Grendel in this castle where Geats slept this night.

Chapter 11

Out in the darkness, the monster stirred, gliding in shadow. Grendel moved quickly through the cloudy night, lurching up from the swampland. The warriors who were to guard the castle slept—all but one. Beowulf, wakeful, was on watch for the demon. His anger mounting, he ached for revenge.

Through the clouds Grendel could see the shining castle. He knew this hall well. Never had he come craving murder, wanting a blood feast, when harder luck and hardier warriors awaited him.

Grendel came to the door and wrenched it open, though the door was bound with iron. His blood lust was great. He raged across the threshold and leapt into the hall. His eyes shone with a fearful evil anger like fire.

There in the hall he saw the warriors, the band of kinsmen, sleeping on the floor. His heart laughed, the evil monster. Grendel thought that before the night ended, he would tear the life from each body, eat them all before the sun rose. The thought of such a feast crazed him. But it was not his fate to feast on mankind after that night.

Beowulf watched his evil steps, waiting to see how the killer Grendel would attack. Beowulf saw the monster's sharp hideous claws rip apart the first Geat warrior to which he came. Grendel bit into muscles, drank the blood from him. In a moment the monster had eaten up the warrior.

Then Grendel moved to another still body, but this one was not sleeping. The monster clutched at Beowulf with his claw. Hand met claw. Grendel sat straight, knowing at once that this he had never encountered: Here was a man whose hand grip was stronger than that of any man on the earth. Nothing could free Grendel from that grip. The monster's mind filled with fear. Grendel longed to flee to his hiding place, to go back to the company of other demons. He had never met a greeting like this in the castle Heorot before.

Beowulf, that brave man, stood straight and stopped the monster's flight. Beowulf tightened his grasp and cracked Grendel's fingers. The monster frantically tried to move; Beowulf clutched Grendel closer. Desperately, the monster tried to wrench himself from Beowulf, wishing himself anywhere else, but Grendel's fingers were in a terrible grip. Grendel was caught. He was trapped. What a miserable journey to the castle this was for the monster!

The two crashed in the hall, sounds of the battle thundering. They raged together, monster and man, and the walls rumbled. The building withstood blow after blow. It was a wonder the castle stood. Inside and out, though, metalworkers had made the walls strong with iron bands.

While the furious fighters battled, many of the mead-benches, covered with gold, reared up from the floor, flew against the walls. None of Hrothgar's wisest men had thought a living creature was strong enough to destroy the hall, to bring down the walls. Only fire's tongues could do that, they thought. Now new, terrible sounds came from the hall, and Danish hearts filled with fear. The sounds were from Grendel, horrible shrieks of pain, anger, and defeat. The Danes shivered in their beds. Beowulf, the strongest man who ever lived, held the monster tight.

Chapter 12

Beowulf had no intention of letting the killer go free. He knew the people of Denmark had no use for the monster. Beowulf's warriors had all leapt from their beds, beloved, ancient swords at the ready, all wanting to be the one to defend their prince. They wanted to cut out Grendel's soul. These warriors did not know when they entered the fight that the best iron in the world, the sharpest blade, could not touch the monster. That evil demon had laid spells that blunted all men's blades.

Yet the monster's time of death had come. His departure from this world was to be wretched. Grendel discovered that he, who had brought so much heart sorrow to the race of men by his murders, could not keep himself alive. Grendel understood that his strength was slipping away, that the man from the Geats had him in his grip. It was hateful to each that the other should live.

The terrible demon had great wounds, and he twisted in pain. A bleeding tear opened in Grendel's shoulder. Muscles split, bones snapped and broke. Beowulf wrenched Grendel's arm from his body. The battle was over. Beowulf had new glory in war. Grendel escaped, wounded, to travel under marshy hills, find his lair and die.

After that bloody battle the Danes rejoiced. Their desires had come to pass. He who had come from afar, Beowulf the bold, had cleansed the castle, made it free from murder and aching grief.

Beowulf rejoiced in his own courage, in his night's work. He had kept his proud boast to the Danes. He had rid the land of the evil sorrow they had so long suffered. Now, in triumph, he nailed high in the rafter Grendel's arm, from hand to shoulder, all there with the claw under the high roof. There was the proof that the monster was dead.

Chapter 13

That morning, crowds surrounded the castle. Princes came from near and from faraway lands to look at the monster's last tracks. Those who examined the trail had no wish to grieve the death of the monster. They followed the bloody tracks of his lonely flight from the castle to the lake of the monsters. In that lake the water boiled with blood, a murky swirl of gore and ooze. The surging bloody waves had covered Grendel's agonizing death. There he hid until he gave up life, and there hell received him.

Home again came the warriors, the young and the old. They turned back from that evil place in happiness, mounted their horses, and rode them back toward the castle. All along the way they retold the story of Beowulf's exploits. Each swore that no other man under heaven was more worthy of being a king. But they found no fault with Hrothgar, their own excellent king.

In their happiness, the warriors let their horses gallop as fast as they wished, the horses racing each other when the road was straight and fast.

Then a poet, one of the king's warriors, began telling the old stories, song after song. He remembered them all. He began to tell Beowulf's praise, tell the tale of his glorious deed; it was a story crafted in smooth verses that bound Beowulf's glory.

He told of Beowulf's bravery, singing the new song alongside the old stories of ancient heroes. He sang of Sigemund's famous deeds of the past—deeds of which the world knew nothing. But Sigemund would tell his nephew Fitela everything as they stood side by side in battle. Together in war they slew a whole tribe of giants with just their two swords. Glory followed Sigemund after his death.

Fitela told how his uncle, Sigemund, had killed a dragon, a jealous keeper of treasure. Sigemund went alone beneath the earth, reckless and brave, and thrust his sword through the dragon, pinning it to the wall. The dragon died in that lightning thrust. Sigemund then went in, gathering the jewels and gold, gathering them at will. Sigemund, the son of Waels, loaded his ship with dragon's treasure and sailed off, the dragon dissolving in his own hot blood.

Sigemund was known to all nations, a hero adventurer, a battle leader. No one had glory like Sigemund. His strength and his treasures grew.

The poet also sang of the king Heremod. Heremod was once the bravest of men, and praises of him were everywhere. But Heremod grew cruel and greedy, and he was betrayed by his own people, who sent him to exile with the Jutes, who killed him.

The poet continued the story of how Heremod's life had turned to misery. His anger and black moods lasted too long; he brought his people sorrow. In earlier days, his people had counted on him, entrusting him with their treasure. They believed that under his strong leadership they would prosper. Heremod's vanity swelled so that he listened only to himself, ignoring his wise counselors. But Beowulf was praised by the poet. Here was a prince who held to his promise, brought his people bright victory.

The Danes raced into the morning light, back to the castle. Many of Hrothgar's people walked to the castle, eager to see the strange trophy in the rafters, eager to sing Beowulf's praise. The king Hrothgar himself walked from his wife's quarters to the castle, his queen beside him. Wealhtheow's attendants came too, walking with them to the noble castle.

Chapter 14

The king Hrothgar stood at the entrance to his castle and stared at the monster's arm dangling in the rafters. "Give thanks to God for this sight! Many terrible attacks have we suffered from Grendel, but God can do wonders. Not long ago, I saw no end to the suffering from this monster. I had given up hope. This castle stood deep in blood, silent, empty. It was a grief that reached deep into my heart, into all our hearts. Not one of my men could keep the terrible monster from our doors.

"Now, Beowulf has come to us, the best of men. The woman who bore such a son into the world, wherever she is, that woman is blessed. Beowulf has done what none of us could. I will love you as a son, Beowulf, and choose you as the son of my hopes. Keep our new kinship forever in your heart. Everything I own you may have. I have given many treasures to much lesser warriors, those poorer at battle. Now you, by yourself, have done a deed that will assure you glory forever and always. Your courage has earned it, and your strength. May God always reward you!"

Then Beowulf spoke, the son of Ecgtheow. "Our hearts were willing and helped our hands perform this work of courage. We risked all against the unknown strength of the monster. I wish, though, that you could have seen the monster Grendel himself, dead here in this castle. I wanted to see him dead, right here. I had plans to bind him hard, clamp him to his deathbed here. The Lord, though did not wish it. I could not hold the monster. However, he left us with his arm, this prize, as he pulled free and ran. He ran with a panicked heart to his death. Grendel was a ferocious monster, terrible in his crimes, but his wound is gaping, and death awaits him. Now our bright God will judge him."

Even Unferth, he who had mocked Beowulf, was humbled into silence. He and all the nobles looked up in the rafters at that arm with its gigantic hand, the fingers ending in nails as hard as steel. Not even the strongest blade could cut through those loathsome claws. Beowulf had done it with his bare hands. The warriors stared at the arm, and they knew Beowulf's strength.

Chapter 15

The king Hrothgar ordered the castle cleaned and furnished. Every man and woman was willing. They hurried to make the great hall ready for a feast. They hung golden tapestries, marvelous paintings in which visitors could take pleasure.

The once-shining castle was badly broken. Iron doors hung from their hinges, and walls buckled despite the iron bands that had bound them. Only the gold-crusted roof remained unharmed when the fiendish monster, stained with his bloody crimes, turned to flee to his death. Nor is death avoided by any of us, try though we may. Each must seek a final resting place where his body will lie.

The banquet hall was ready, and Hrothgar made his way there, ready for feasting and peace. Never has there been a better victory celebration. Hrothgar was a famous host, and the hall was filled with good friends. The warriors lined the benches, rejoicing.

King Hrothgar gave Beowulf a golden banner of war to signal the victory. He gave him a golden helmet and mail shirt that glittered with jewels, a jewel-encrusted sword. All these were laid before Beowulf, who was happy to be praised, pleased to be richly rewarded for his deeds.

Never had a king given another man four such fine treasures. The helmet was bound with bands of metal, bands that would protect Beowulf from shining blades swung against it.

Then the king of the Danes called for attention and eight horses entered the hall. Each had a golden bridle. One of the horses had a jeweled saddle—it had been Hrothgar's, his war seat. It had carried the king when he rode to war; his bravery was always famous, even in the heat of battle, with the dead falling around him. To Beowulf Hrothgar gave this jeweled war seat, commanding him to use the gifts well. Hrothgar repaid Beowulf's bravery with these gifts and earned praise from those who knew the truth.

Chapter 16

Hrothgar offered still more gifts to Beowulf's warriors. He gave each a treasure, ancient swords and armor. For the Geatish warrior Grendel had killed, Hrothgar paid gold. The king knew that the monster would have killed many more had not God, and Beowulf, changed that fate. The Lord ruled then, as he does now, and our hearts must seek out his will. The world has both good and evil, and those who are in the world meet both.

Now there was rejoicing and song before the king. The sound of the harp filled the hall, verses of poetry sung. Then Hrothgar's poet came to tell another of the ancient tales—the famous story of Finn's sons.

Now hear the poet's story of Finn and his death.

The poet told the story from the beginning, when Hnaef of the Danes was attacked with no warning by Finn's people, the Frisians, who had come to Denmark. The Frisians killed half of the Danes, and they killed the Danish king Hnaef.

Finn's wife Hildeburh was Hnaef's sister. That was a mournful woman. She wept for her dead brother, King Hnaef, and for her son, also killed in the battle. She wept under the skies where she had had her greatest joy. Both were men she dearly loved.

Most of the Finns, too, had been killed. There were not enough left to conquer the Danes or to force Hnaef's prince, Hengest, to flee his castle. Neither side could win, and the fighting stalled.

Finn of the Frisians offered terms for peace. There would be no victory; instead, the two warring tribes would share the Danes' castle. When gifts of treasure were given, they would be shared equally. On both sides, they agreed to keep the peace. Finn swore that he and the Dane Hengest would live like brothers. Neither would plot in secret against the other, even though the Danes would be living with Finn, who had killed their king. The Danes now had no king—and no choice. Finn swore that if his warriors brought up the painful past, his sword would silence them.

Hnaef was ready on the funeral pyre,[7] dressed in gold. The others who had died lay with him. They were many, their mail shirts crusted with blood, the shine of gold and gore mingled. Many had fallen. Hildeburh sadly gave her son's body to the fire, to lie next to his uncle. The flames rose and the queen wept. The king of the Danes, Hnaef, was lifted into place on the fire. Smoke curled to the heavens, logs spit and roared, and the greedy fire swallowed up the bones and blood of all. Their glory was gone.

Chapter 17

The poet then told of Finn's warriors who survived and returned home. Hengest lived that hard winter through in Friesland with Finn, whom he hated. He had no choice. Hengest longed to return to Denmark, but he could not return. Wind whirled the choppy seas and the cold hands of winter froze the water. The waves froze in place until the winter ended.

Then winter was gone, the fields green and lush. Hengest left Friesland, thinking more of vengeance than of returning to his home. He wanted to settle the bitter feud with Finn. He could not forget Finn's

---

7. **funeral pyre** a pile of wood on which a body is burned during a funeral ceremony

deeds and his bloody sword. Hengest made plans, and made them again. Then a Danish soldier dropped a sword into Hengest's lap. It was a sword that Finn and his warriors knew and feared; it was the finest of blades.

The time had come. Hengest drove that sword deep into Finn's belly, killing the king in his own castle. The other Danes rose, still enraged with Finn's earlier treachery, and the misery he had caused. Their swords were eager. The hall grew red with the blood of Frisians, and the Danes took their queen. They stripped the castle of riches, fine tapestries, gold. The Danes carried the queen Hildeburh back to the Danes, her people.

The poet finished his song of the Finns, and his listeners laughed and drank. Then queen Wealhtheow came forward, dressed in glistening gold, to the king and his nephew Hrothulf. Unferth sat at Hrothgar's feet. All knew his great courage, although he had killed his brothers.

Wealhtheow spoke then to her husband, King Hrothgar. "Take this cup, my treasure-giving king. Offer the Geats your kind words, as a wise king should. Be generous with them. Give them the treasure your armies have brought from all corners of the earth. I know you think of Beowulf as your son. Your castle stands strong because of him. Heorot has been cleansed. Be generous while you have these riches to share. My king, your nephew Hrothulf would rule the young warriors well if you should die before him. I know he would want to treat our sons well. He will remember how we treated him when he was young, his father dead and he but a child."

Then Wealhtheow turned to where her sons were. Beowulf was seated between them. Walking across the hall, she seated herself by their side.

Chapter 18

Then a cup was offered Beowulf in kind friendship and taken that way. The Danes gave him bracelets of twisted gold, a shirt of mail, other garments, and the largest gold necklace ever seen on this earth. No better treasures were known under Heaven. Cheers for Beowulf arose throughout the hall.

Then Wealhtheow spoke to Beowulf before all the assembled company. "Wear this necklace, and these jewels, my dear young Beowulf. Grow richer, and may your fortunes and your fame grow. May you have every success. Make your strength known, and serve as a leader to the young boys here. I will never forget your kindness. Forever, all men shall praise you. While you live, may your courage buy you peace! Be kind to my sons in your great strength—be a hero to them. Each warrior at this feast is faithful to his lord and to each other. They are united, a nation prepared, and will do as I ask."

She went to her seat. It was a glorious feast. They drank rare wine. Little did they know the fate that awaited them that night after Hrothgar went to his bed. A number of men stayed in the hall as they had many years before, drinking and cheering. They cleared the benches and made beds and pillows. They could not know that one of them was doomed as he lay down to sleep.

At his head each warrior placed his round battle shield, made of bright wood. By each was his helmet, his mail shirt, his great spear made of wood. It was always their custom to be ready for war, whether they were at home or in battle. They always wanted to be ready to defend their king, if needed. They were good warriors.

Chapter 19

The warriors sank into sleep. One paid dearly for his rest that night. He was like all the others before him who had died when Grendel had come raging in the night, until that monster had met his death. Soon men came to know that while one monster had died, another still lived and meant to get her revenge. Grendel's monstrous mother was miserable. She had dwelled in the murky, icy lake since Cain had killed his brother with an angry sword. God had cast Cain's kind into the wastelands. Grendel was one of those angry monsters, who had found at Heorot a brave warrior who ended his life. Grendel had gone away in agony to seek his death in the dark lake.

Now Grendel's mother, enraged by the death of her son, plotted her revenge. Her sorrow and mourning were as great as her towering rage. She came to Heorot that night where the Danish warriors slept peacefully. Her strength was only less terrible than her son's in the way a woman's strength is less than a man's.

Then in the hall were swords drawn, many shields raised high. None had time to dress in mail shirts, to think of helmets, when the surprise attack came. The warriors rose against her, their swords flashing. The monster's only thought was to escape with her life. Quickly she snared a warrior with her sharp claws, snatched him from his bed. Then she fled to her terrible home in the moor, beneath the dark lake.

The warrior she had taken was the one dearest to Hrothgar of all those in his wide kingdom. He was a man rich in fame. The monster had killed a glorious warrior, cut short his life.

Beowulf was not there. He had been given a bed of honor in another building. Then all Heorot rang with outrage. She had taken the bloody arm of Grendel that had hung high in the castle rafters. Grief had returned to Denmark. Each side in the terrible battle had paid with the life of a loved one.

The king trembled with grief when he learned of the death of his warrior, his dearest friend dead. Hrothgar quickly sent for Beowulf. In the darkness before dawn, Beowulf came with his warriors to the king. Hrothgar wondered if God ever planned to end his misery.

The Geats came quickly into the castle, their footsteps echoing in the silent hall. Beowulf crossed the floor to talk to the king, to ask if the night had passed quickly and if all was well.

Chapter 20

"Do not speak of happiness!" Hrothgar answered. "We Danes are destined to misery. Aeschere is dead, my most trusted friend, the man I relied on for wise advice, my companion in battle. Whatever a friend should be, Aeschere was. Now another monster has come and found him in Heorot, murdered him. That slaughtering spirit has taken his body I know not where. She has now had her revenge for the killing of Grendel.

"Last night you killed that monster, because too long had he destroyed my people. Grendel fell in that battle, his life over. Now another has come, in righteous evil, to avenge her son. She is a monster willing and determined to bring us more sorrow. So it must seem to my warriors, who are now mourning their companion, a man who treated them all nobly."

Hrothgar continued to speak to Beowulf. "I have heard of my people, workers in the fields, who have seen a pair of monsters wandering in the moors and marshes. They are giant fiends living in those barren lands. So far as any of the workers could tell, one was misshapen, but in the shape of a woman. The other was deformed, with a manlike shape, but larger than any warrior anyone had ever seen. In long ago days, the people named him Grendel. No one knows who gave birth to these monsters, or where they are from. They live secretly in a dark land. Theirs is the land where wolves live, where winds howl, with gloomy caves. In that land a stream goes down under the dark hills and floods under the earth to form a lake.

"That fearsome lake is not far from here, measured in miles. The black lake lies hidden, overhung with roots. At water's edge are frost-bound trees. Their roots snake into the water, keeping it dark. At night that lake burns like a torch—it is a terrible wonder. There is no wise man who lives who knows the bottom of that black lake, that home of monsters. Even though the deer may be chased down by hounds, full of despair, that deer would rather be attacked on the shore than plunge into that black lake. It is not a pleasant place!

"Waves angrily smash against the shores. The wind stirs fierce, gloomy storms until the air is filled with choking dust and the heavens weep. Once again, we seek your help. You are our only hope. The home of these water fiends is not far from here. Find it if you dare! If you go, I will reward you richly, as I did before, with ancient treasure. Wealth will be yours if you win this battle!"

Chapter 21

Beowulf answered Hrothgar. "Do not grieve, wise king. It is better to seek revenge than to mourn. Every man must come to the end of his life, and it is better to win fame before we die. Fame after death is the noblest of goals.

"Come, good guardian, let us go quickly to find the tracks of that murderous beast. I will promise you that the monster will find no safety in the depths of the earth, nor in the wooded mountains, nor in the bottom of the sea. She may go where she will—she will not live for long! Have patience for one more day of misery—that is all I ask."

The gray-haired king leaped to his feet and gave thanks to God for Beowulf's words. Hrothgar called for a horse to be saddled for him, his curly-haired steed of war. The wise Hrothgar rode in kingly fashion. His shield-bearing soldiers marched with him.

They followed the monster's tracks through the forest. The fiend's huge tracks were easy to follow on the narrow path. She had traveled straight toward her dark home over wild moors, through wandering streams. With her she had the body of Hrothgar's friend, the best friend he had.

The king led his troop of warriors onto a narrow path where horses could go only one at a time. They went up slopes that were steep and rocky, down slippery cliffs where sea monsters and dragons swam in watery caves.

Then, with a few brave warriors, Hrothgar went to spy what was ahead. Where gnarled clumps of trees bent against cold gray stones, they came to a bleak wood surrounding a bloody lake. The warriors were silent at the sight before them. At the edge of that hellish swamp was Aeschere's head. Black water surged around it, and the water boiled with blood and hot gore. The Danes' war horns sounded a mournful sound, again and again.

The warriors laid down their weapons. They could see the water below crawling with snakes, dragons swimming in the gore. On the slopes black monsters lay curled. With the morning light, they would slither through the water. They were the sea beasts and serpents that follow travelers on the sea.

When they heard the cries of the war horn, the beasts left the shore, swollen with rage. Beowulf raised his bow, and shot one of those swimming monsters. The lifeblood of the great serpent seeped away as the arrow sank deep into its body. Before the dying monster could escape, more warriors hooked its thrashing body and dragged it to shore. There they looked in awe at the monster from the deep. It was covered with horrible scales. They watched it blacken with death.

Then Beowulf called for his armor. He had no fear. Beowulf's mail shirt was strong and wellmade. He knew it would protect him from a foe's blow to his heart. A gleaming helmet protected his head. The helmet was rich with gold and worked with jewels, made by ancient metal workers with wondrous skills. No sword or ax could bite through that metal.

Perhaps his strongest support was the sword, Hrunting, which Hrothgar had loaned Beowulf. It was given by Unferth. Hrunting was one of the oldest of the kingdom's treasures. Its iron edge was hardened in war blood. Never had it failed any man who knew how to use it. Once again, Hrunting was called upon to do a deed of great courage.

When he gave Beowulf the sword, Unferth did not mention his first words of challenge to Beowulf. Unferth did not dare to risk his life under bloody waves. He was not brave enough. It was then he lost his glory and his name for bold deeds. That was not so with Beowulf. He was armed and prepared for battle.

Chapter 22

The brave Beowulf spoke. "Hrothgar, son of Healfdene, wisest of men, remember what you said in the warmth of the castle. If I fall in battle, you shall be the father to my companions, be their guardian. If I die, Hrothgar, send the treasure you have given me to my king Hygelac. When he gazes on those riches he will know that I found in Denmark a noble king whose favor I won. Also be sure that Unferth is given my famous old sword, a hard-edged blade. With Hrunting I shall find glory, or death will take me."

After he had spoken, the man of the Geats turned away. He would not wait for an answer and he went to his fate. He walked into the surging, bloody water. For most of a day, he sank through the water, until he saw the mud of the bottom.

Soon the water monster came to discover who would explore her bleak devils' home. She groped for him, and then she snatched up Beowulf in her terrible claws. Tear though she might, Beowulf's armor protected him. She could not stab his heart.

Then the black water monster bore him away, dragged Beowulf to her underwater den. So tight was her grip that Beowulf could not draw his sword. As she carried him deeper, strange sea fiends tore at his mail shirt, crunched their teeth on his armor, all greedy for Beowulf's blood.

Then Beowulf saw the monster had dragged him to a cold chamber where no water could reach. It was roofed against flood water, far beneath the earth. In that terrible cavern, the light of flames licked at the walls.

Beowulf then saw the sea witch who had taken him so deep. He thrust at her with his sword, straight at her head. The iron sang its song of blood, sang of Beowulf's strength. But the water monster discovered that Hrunting could not cut her evil hide. The edge would not bite. Hrunting failed Beowulf, though so often before it had triumphed in battle. It was the first time a word could be said against Hrunting's glory.

Beowulf's courage did not fail. Angry, he flung away the useless iron, far across the cave. It lay on the ground, bejeweled, bright-edged. What Beowulf did trust was his own strength. He remembered how he had grappled with Grendel and brought him down. If weapons were useless, he would use his hands. So does a man act who cares only to win the battle, and not for his own life.

The leader of the Geats did not shrink from the fight. He seized Grendel's mother in his mighty hands, twisting her arms with angry strength. Beowulf bent her backwards to the floor. The sea witch clamped his arms in her cold claws and crushed him so he stumbled in weariness. In an instant, she forced him to the ground.

There, Grendel's mother straddled Beowulf's body and drew her broad knife high above her to strike at the killer of her only son. Then the woven armor saved Beowulf as she plunged the knife down. The blade struck him harmlessly. The mail shirt kept Beowulf from death. The wise Lord decided that Beowulf should live and rise again to fight.

Chapter 23

Then Beowulf saw glittering there a blade bright with victory. It had been made by the giants. Its edge was sharp, the knife an honor for the warrior who held it. It was a blade for a hero. The sword gleamed with gold and jewels, so heavy that no other man besides Beowulf could have carried it.

Beowulf seized the giant's sword with both hands. He raised the gleaming gold handle high in anger. There was rage in his heart. Beowulf swung it at the she-monster's neck, swung it so angrily it burst through her neck, breaking the bone rings there.

Her body in halves, Grendel's mother fell to the ground, dead. The sword was wet with blood, and the hero rejoiced.

Suddenly a bright light blazed from above, as light will come from heaven. Beowulf looked about himself, as he moved along the wall, his weapon raised. Beowulf was still in a fury. Even now, the blade was not idle. The warrior could still find a use for it. Beowulf meant to find Grendel and repay him for every bloody death he had caused. There were so many more than the 15 Beowulf had seen slaughtered that night in Heorot, another 15 carried to the foul monster's nest. For 12 long years Grendel had murdered Hrothgar's companions, massacred them as they slept, swallowed and eaten them.

Now, Beowulf could pay Grendel back. He saw the body of the monster lying there, armless and lifeless from the battle with Beowulf. With a fierce, angry swing, Beowulf struck the dead monster through the neck, chopping off his head.

Above, on shore, the warriors were watching the lake. Suddenly, with anxious hearts, they saw a great surge of blood and gore come from below. Broken down with grief, the Danes talked quietly about the deeds of the brave Geat. They did not think they would see him return. They agreed upon it. The she-monster had destroyed Beowulf. Never again would he return to the living, come back as proud as he had left.

The sun sank low. Sadly, the Danes left the boiling lake of blood. They carried a sorrowful message to their king. The grieving Danes sought to comfort each other and their king at the castle. Only their guests, the Geats, stayed on at the edge of the wood, staring sick with horror at the boiling blood. They wished without hope that their hero might appear.

Beowulf looked around him at the treasure, heaped and glittering, in the evil cavern under the lake. He wanted nothing more from that dark hall except the handle of the giant's sword, and Grendel's head.

In that she-monster's lair, the giant's sword had begun to melt into battle-bloody icicles. It was a wondrous thing to watch. It was like the melting of ice in the spring. The monster's blood was too hot for the blade, and the spirit that had died then too poisonous.

Soon Beowulf was swimming straight up to the light, that hero who had withstood the attacks of two fearsome monsters and killed them both. He shot up through the water. As he rose, the monster spirits were cleansed from the lake. The alien spirit had finished her evil days and this fleeting life. The peaceful pond was opened to sunlight.

Then Beowulf, that brave protector of sea travelers, swam to the land. He was joyful, carrying his heavy burdens of sword handle and monster head. His fellow Geats came to greet him, overcome with thanks to God for returning their leader safe after his fight with that monster of death. They unbuckled Beowulf's mail shirt and helmet from him and turned to walk to Heorot. Behind them the lake was thick with the monsters' blood, still rising to the surface.

The warriors marched, glad-hearted, away from that place. They followed the narrow trail, reached familiar ground. Brave as kings, men carried Grendel's head from that place. Four warriors struggled with the huge trophy, that head raised high on a war spear. Still, the warriors were proud of their grisly prize, and they determined that the Danes should see it. At last they came to the door of Heorot, 14 of them, marching in triumph. Beowulf marched among them, proud of his warriors.

Then the Geats' great warrior, Beowulf, entered the hall covered with glory for his fierce fighting. He sought Hrothgar, and greeted him by dragging Grendel's head across the floor. He brought it straight to where Hrothgar sat with his queen. It was a terrible and wondrous sight, and the warriors stared at it. Then Beowulf, son of Ecgtheow, spoke. "Behold, Hrothgar, the gift from the sea the joyful Geats have brought you. I almost lost my life, fighting for it, struggling under the water. I would have certainly been dead, and that she monster victorious, had not God been with me."

Chapter 24

"The noble sword, Hrunting," continued Beowulf, "was of no use in that continued battle, but is it ready for many more. The good Lord helped me see a bright sword hanging on the wall, an heirloom from the giants. When the time was right, I lifted that weapon, swung it, and killed the sea monster in her own home. After the sword had sliced through her neck, ending her life and her misery, that blade began to melt. The dark, evil blood melted the blade. I have brought you the handle of that ancient sword.

"The monsters are gone forever, banished from Heorot. I promise you that tonight the Danes will sleep without care. Everyone—all your warriors, your women and children—may rest peacefully without fear of any monster, mother or son."

Then Beowulf gave the strange golden hilt, the handle of the giants' sword, to Hrothgar. After being in the possession of monsters, the sword had come into the hands of the best of the kings in Scandinavia.

Hrothgar was gladdened, and he gazed at the hilt, this great treasure of old. There upon it was engraved the story of past wars. The story told of the time the flood drowned the race of giants, and how they suffered, and how they were a people strange to God. The flood was God's last payment to them for their deeds. Hrothgar saw on the hilt the runic letters[8] that spelled the name of the one for whom the sword had been made. The handle was finely worked, made with twisted gold and ornamented with carvings of serpents.

Then Hrothgar spoke, and the people were silent. "What I say, I say from a lifetime of experience. I am a man who remembers our past. This prince Beowulf was born for glory. Beowulf, my friend, your fame spreads far across the waters, wherever men travel. You hold that fame wisely, are patient with your strength and with our weakness. I will keep my promises to you. Now your counsel must be to your Geat friends, not to my people. You will bring courage to their hearts through all the years you live.

"Beware of becoming like Heremod, who brought his people great sorrow. In his mad rages he killed his own warriors—the very people who ate at his table! Instead of treasure, he gave his warriors misery. At the end he ravaged his people until hate cut him off from all joy. His people fled from him and he was alone, even though God had raised him up to be a leader of his people. Learn from his example, understand what a king must be.

---

8. **runic letters** letters of an ancient language

"Our Lord has granted some men wisdom, others riches, others land. He has power over all things. Sometimes God gives a king land, such wide holdings. The king cannot see that there will ever be an end to his good fortune. Happily he goes from feast to feast. His life is lived amongst plenty; illness in no way troubles him; there is no war to cause him to sharpen his blade."

Chapter 25

"Then," continued King Hrothgar, "his pride and arrogance increase. His soul and his conscience slumber. While they sleep, a killer draws a bow and shoots an arrow into the king's heart. It is a bitter arrow, containing the dark commands of a wicked devil. No armor can withstand that arrow.

"Now what has pleased the king no longer does. His greed grows. He gives no treasure to his loyal warriors. What he has had seems too little. He no longer is thankful to God for his health, or his life, or his fortune. Then it happens: The body God has lent him begins to fail. When he dies, his body burns on the pyre, disappears in a swirl of smoke, and he is gone.

"Then another steps up to take his place and pass out his treasure, turning the dead king's greed to reward. No one mourns the fallen king. Guard against this curse, beloved Beowulf! Do not turn to pride. Your fame and strength live now—this is your time. Soon, though, sickness will come, or war. A plunging spear may end your happiness, or surging waves, or the bite of a knife. Death will come, faster than you know. No one can escape it.

"I have ruled the Danes for half a century, shielded them, protected them from war with my strength. I ruled so well that I had no enemies on earth. But I was not safe. Happiness left my land. Joy turned to grief when the monster Grendel, careless murderer, came to Heorot. I suffered through his hatred.

"Now, thanks be to God for deliverance from this long heartache. Now, with my own eyes, I can look at Grendel's huge bloody head. But now, Beowulf, sit. It is time to feast and drink with your companions, to take honor in your battle. When morning comes, I will share with you the treasures of this land."

Gladdened, Beowulf took his seat at the table, as the wise king Hrothgar asked. Around him were his trusted warriors. Bright laughter rang throughout the hall, and sounds of victory, as servants passed cups of ale to Geats and Danes alike, all those famed for their courage. This second feast had as many delights as the first.

Night fell, the dark shadows creeping up the wall, and Hrothgar called for sleep, for silence, and peace. Beowulf, weary to his soul, went to his bed and sank gratefully into slumber. Once more he was a guest in that mighty castle. The Danes' servants, thoughtful of Beowulf's needs, spread covers over him.

Then Beowulf, the great-hearted one, rested. The great castle rose above him, its golden spires gleaming. He slept until the cry of a black-feathered raven woke him. The bird's cheerful song announced the break of day. Beowulf and his warriors prepared to return to their people. They would set sail for their far land. They would hope to see it soon.

Before they set sail, Beowulf bid Unferth to take back Hrunting, that great sword. Beowulf thanked Unferth for the loan of the weapon, called it a good friend in war, and did not blame its edges for failure in the last battle.

The Geats yearned to be gone. The warriors were ready in their armor. Beowulf then walked to the throne where Hrothgar was sitting in kingly glory. Beowulf saluted him.

Chapter 26

Beowulf spoke. "Now we voyagers who came from afar wish to seek our own king again. We have been treated well here and entertained splendidly. You have brought for us everything we could possibly ask. If ever I can do anything on earth for you—help you in sickness or sorrow, fight your battles—summon me. I will return. If I hear, from my home across the ocean, that men dwelling near here threaten your kingdom, as some before have, I will bring 1,000 warriors to your aid. I know my king Hygelac stands behind me. If I need his help to aid you, he will give it. He will lend our strength, battle-sharp weapons to shield you and help you. And if your oldest son, Hrethric, decides to visit the land of the Geats, he will find many friends there. An able warrior from a strong land is always welcome."

Hrothgar replied, "The Lord must have placed those words in your mind. I have never heard one so young speak so wisely. You are strong in body, bold in actions, wealthy in thought. If your king Hygelac should ever die in battle, and you live, the Geats could not choose a more able king, a better keeper of treasure. Your character pleases me more the more you stay with us, Beowulf. You have brought peace to both our peoples, turned Geats and Danes into brothers. There is no thought of war, of anger and hatred, as in the old days. As long as I am king, we shall send you treasures. Many a seafaring Dane will greet his fellow Geats with good gifts as they cross paths in the sea. Your people live by the old ways, as we do. The hearts of the Geats are forever open to their friends, but closed against their enemies."

Then Hrothgar, that good king of a noble race, embraced Beowulf. Tears ran down his face and streaked his gray beard. It seemed to them both, the warrior from the Geats and the noble king, that they would not meet again in this life. Admiration for Beowulf welled in Hrothgar's heart, and his heart swelled with regret that Beowulf would sail so far away.

And then Beowulf left Hrothgar, left the castle. The prince dressed in gold walked across the green grass to his ship, his arms heaped high with treasure. Beowulf was proud of the gifts Hrothgar had given him.

The noble ship awaited its master and then set sail. The journey back to the land of the Geats was filled with talk of the generosity of the king Hrothgar. That was a noble king, blameless until old age stole from him the joy of his strength. This is the fate of many.

Chapter 27

The band of Geats, young and bold, marched in their armor down to the shore, where they had first come. The coast watcher was there again, as he had been when they arrived. He watched as their metal armor glistened in the sun. This time he did not greet them roughly, but he rode toward them eagerly. The coast watcher hailed them with cheerful greetings, and he made them welcome. The warriors would be welcome in their home country, he declared.

On the beach, the ship was laden with war gear. It sat heavy with treasure and horses. The mast stood high over the hoard of gold—first Hrothgar's, and now theirs. Beowulf rewarded the boat's watchman, who had stayed behind, by giving him a sword bound with gold. The weapon would bring the watchman honor.

The ship felt the wind and left the cliffs of Denmark. They traveled in deep water, the wind fierce and straining at the sails, making the deck timbers creak. No hindrance stopped the ship as it boomed through the sea, skimmed on the water, winged over waves. Then the lands of home were before them, the sea cliffs of Geatland that they knew. Driven by the strong wind, the ship rammed high onto the beach. There on the shore was the harbor guard, who ran to meet them. They had long waited for the warriors' arrival, scanned the ocean, watched for the men coming from afar.

Quickly, the broad ship was moored to the beach by strong ropes so high waves could not pull the boat loose and tear it away. Beowulf ordered the treasures, the gold, the gems, unloaded and carried to Hygelac, their king. They did not have far to go. Hygelac was at home in his castle near the sea. There he stayed with his warriors.

Hygelac was a famous king, with a splendid castle and a wife, Hygd, who was young and yet wise beyond her age. She was a generous queen.

Chapter 28

Beowulf went marching with his army of warriors from the sea. Above them the world-candle shone bright from the south. They had survived the sea journey, and now they went in quickly to where they knew their protector, king Hygelac, lived with his warriors and shared his treasure.

Hygelac was told of their arrival, that Beowulf had come home. Benches were quickly readied to receive the warriors and their leader Beowulf. Hygelac now sat, ready to greet them in his court.

Then Beowulf sat down with Hygelac, the nephew with his uncle. Hygelac offered words of welcome, and Beowulf greeted his king with loyal words. Hygd, Hygelac's queen, moved through the hall, bringing cups of ale she herself served to the warriors.

Anxious to learn what had happened, Hygelac asked Beowulf for news of his trip. "What luck did you have, Beowulf, when you left on that long voyage, seeking adventure at the castle Heorot? Did you ease the well-known heartache of Hrothgar, the king? Your journey lay heavy on my heart—I was afraid to let you go to him. For a long time I made you stay here, forcing the Danes to fight their own fight against the monster Grendel. I now give thanks to God that I see you here, unharmed!"

Beowulf, Ecgtheow's brave son, spoke. "My lord, my famous meeting with Grendel is a secret to no one in Denmark. They all know of the nighttime battle I fought with the monster. That hell demon ruled in darkness with death and warriors' grief through many long years. I rid the world of the monster, ended his reign. I avenged his crimes so completely that no kin of Grendel will ever boast otherwise.

"Then I went to the castle Heorot to greet the king, Hrothgar. When he learned what I had done, he gave me a seat between his sons. In Heorot, there were sounds of victory, shouts of vengeance. Never have I seen a greater feast. His famous queen Wealhtheow, keeper of the peace, walked through the hall cheering the warriors and offering them gifts of rings and bracelets."

Chapter 29

"But I will tell you more of my fight with Grendel. When heaven's gem, the sun, glided under the earth, the angry monster came to that mighty castle. We were all waiting. First, the monster seized Hondscioh the Geat, who was sleeping in his armor. Grendel snatched him up, tore him apart, crunched him greedily, swallowed him, that poor doomed warrior.

"Grendel had only begun his bloody night. He meant to leave us with his belly full. Next, the monster tested my strength. We went hand to hand. Dangling by his side was an empty bag, a huge bag sewn from a dragon's skin and made with the skill of a devil. The clasps were cunningly made. Grendel meant to put me in that bag when our fight was over and save me for another meal. The monster was strong and bold. His war claw seized me. I waited no longer but went to greet him, grabbing his arm. I stood firmly and his strength was useless. It failed him."

Chapter 30

"The whole story of the battle with Grendel is too long to tell," Beowulf said. "With my actions, my lord, I won some honor for our people. Grendel and I grappled, and the monster managed to escape and cling to life for a time—but he left behind his arm, which we nailed high to the rafters. Soon after, Grendel died at the bottom of the dark lake, in pain and misery.

"Hrothgar, the king of the Danes, rewarded me with gold and treasures for this work. We sat down to a feast, and there was song and laughter. Hrothgar told of the old days; at times he struck a harp in joy and at other times told of high victories or times of his youth that were both true and sorrowful. Sometimes he wept, the old king, remembering what he had done, what he had seen, and what he had learned. In that castle, Heorot, we spent the day, enjoying our ease, until night fell.

"That night, Grendel's mother rose quickly from the dark lake to take her revenge. Her son had been killed, and she wanted those who had done it to pay. She burst into Heorot and snatched up a warrior—as it happens, she chose Aeschere. When morning came, the Danes were not even able to place their beloved friend on the funeral pyre. She had borne the body away to her hellish home in the lake.

"The death of Aeschere was the bitterest for Hrothgar. He had wept for many of his warriors, dead by Grendel's hand, but of all his warriors, Aeschere was the closest to him. It was then that Hrothgar asked me to once again seek glory, this time by plunging into that evil water to search for the one who had done this. He promised me great rewards.

"I dove down, found the keeper of the terrible deep. We fought hand to hand, Grendel's mother and I. The lake seethed in blood. Then I cut off the head of Grendel's mother in that hall of death, using a giant's huge sword. I barely escaped with my life—my death was not yet written. The king of the Danes, Hrothgar, kept his promise, and heaped treasures at my feet."

Chapter 31

"Hrothgar lived as a good king must. He gave me treasures of my own choosing. Now I wish, good king, to bring them to you, to show my goodwill. All my joys depend on you. My life is at your service. Few kin have I left on this earth, and none closer than you, my king." So Beowulf spoke.

Beowulf then brought in the golden banner, the gold-handled sword, the hand-linked mail shirt that had been given to him. Beowulf said, "Hrothgar gave me these gifts. He said that I should tell you from where these treasures came. King Heorogar, Hrothgar's older brother, was king until he died and Hrothgar took the throne. Heorogar kept this finery, would not give it to his own son, even though the son had proven his loyalty. And now, these are yours. May they serve you well!"

After the gleaming battle prizes came four swift horses, all alike. Beowulf had brought his king horses and treasures. This is how a brave warrior should act, and not weave nets of evil in secret, or plan the death of his companions. King Hygelac kept faith with his nephew, and each worked for the other's success.

Next, Beowulf gave queen Hygd the necklace, that wonderfully wrought treasure that Wealhtheow had given him. After that time, the shining gold necklace adorned her. To the queen he also gave three horses, with golden saddles.

Thus Beowulf showed himself not only as a man brave in battle, but of good deeds. He did not kill his companions in drunken rages. His heart was not savage. He guarded the precious gift that God had given him, strength, and used it only in war—and then, bravely.

And yet when he was a child no good was thought of Beowulf. The Geats thought he was worthless. When he sat with them in their hall, the king gave him no gifts. The other warriors thought his use was little. He had no champions among the heroes. They suspected he was a coward, lazy and slow. Change came to Beowulf as he climbed to manhood. He gained courage and strength in war.

Then Hygelac brought in Beowulf's grandfather's great sword, worked in gold. None of the Geats could boast a more noble weapon. Hygelac laid the sword in Beowulf's lap, and he gave him seven thousand units of land, houses and all. The land of the Geats was home to both Hygelac and Beowulf. Both had much land, but Hygelac, who was king, had more. Together the two kept the country together in friendship.

In later days it happened that after a fierce battle, Hygelac lay dead. His son, Heardred, was killed in war by the Swedes, who had sought Heardred in his own land. After that dark time, the kingdom came into Beowulf's hand, and he ruled.

Beowulf was the king 50 winters. He was a wise king, a good guardian of the land. By then he was an old ruler. Then, in the dark night a flame dragon awoke from its dark dreams to bring terror to Beowulf's people. The dragon had slept in a huge stone mound, with a secret entrance below, unknown to men. One day a wanderer stumbled on it and discovered the ancient treasure, all the jewels and gold the dragon had been guarding.

The man reached out to the treasure and took a shining cup, adorned with jewels. The dragon, which was sleeping, was tricked by the silence of the thief. After discovering the theft, the dragon swelled with rage. It swept through the land, and all of Geatland knew the dragon's anger.

Chapter 32

The wanderer had not come intending to steal. He was a thief not from desire, but need. He was a slave who had been beaten by his masters. He had escaped, and run from his masters. The slave had gone to the stone mound searching for shelter.

When the slave saw the dragon, his heart was filled with horror. Not wanting to wake the dragon, the slave, terror-stricken, turned and ran for safety, but he grabbed one cup to give to his masters, to help the slave beg for mercy.

The dragon's hoard was filled high with treasure, hidden there by the last warrior of a noble race. The ancient riches of his people were left in the darkness as the end of his race came. They had died one by one in battle, and the last warrior watched them, knowing he was next. The gold and jewels the warrior had guarded for so long would not bring him pleasure much longer.

The warrior brought the treasures to a stone tower built near the sea, below a cliff. The fortress was sealed. It had no windows and no doors. Waves were in front of it, and rocks behind.

The last warrior spoke, but to no one. "Earth, I return to you what was once yours. These treasures belong to men now gone into silence. War-death has taken my people too young. Where once was bright servants to shine the ale cups? No one is left to lift the swords. No one leads, no one follows. The coat of mail, which has stood attack after attack, rusts as its warrior decays. There is no singing, no sound of the harp. Evil death has taken everything."

So he spoke, sadly, of those who had died. The last warrior lived from day to day, without joy, until at last death came for him. Then, in the night, the dragon that flies wrapped in flame came in search of a cave. Instead, it found gold. There the dragon that men fear stayed, burying itself in the mounds of gold and jewels, unable to use it, but unable to abandon such a treasure hoard.

For 300 years the dragon guarded the treasure and dwelt there in the earth. The dragon had fierce powers, but it slumbered until a single man kindled its fury. The slave stole a jeweled cup and bought his delighted master's forgiveness. The slave was pardoned, the master marveling at the ancient work on the cup. But the hoard had been robbed, its treasure taken and the dragon awakened.

In fury, the dragon slithered and sniffed, and finally spotted the slave's footprint along the stone walls. The slave had survived in his mission, come close enough to the dragon to touch its scaly head, marvel at its huge jaws. Yet the slave had lived, through the grace of God—and a pair of swift feet.

Quickly the dragon moved, anxious to find the man who had done him this grave injury. The dragon searched all around the stone tower, but it found no trace of the man. The slave had run too fast. The forest was empty. The dragon went back to its tower, plotting bloody revenge. Then he saw what was missing from his splendid treasure. Restless, the dragon waited until night fell. He would avenge that jeweled cup with the blood of men.

When the sun was gone, the dragon's heart was glad. It flew across the land, burning with its fire breath, wild with anger. Now only sorrow faced those on land, and worse for their great king.

Chapter 33

The dragon began to spew flames, which burned down the people's homes. The Geats watched in horror as the flames rose. The deadly flying worm meant to leave nothing alive. Across the land, the flickering signs of its hatred were everywhere. How the destroyer hated the Geats! Before dawn, the dragon would wing back to its hoard of treasure. It had burned everything of the Geats. Now it trusted in the stone walls around it to protect it. In this, it was wrong.

Beowulf came to know the terror. The dragon burned Beowulf's home, his beloved castle, melted it in surging flames. The burning was the greatest of sorrows to the king. Somehow, Beowulf felt he had offended God. That was why his castle was destroyed. His thoughts were dark, which was unusual for him.

The dragon had burned the land along the sea near the castle as well as the castle, the people's protection on the shore. The dragon had destroyed the heart of the country. For that, the king Beowulf planned revenge. He commanded that a special shield be made for him— one of nothing but iron. Well did Beowulf know that the usual shield, made of linden wood, would be of no use to him against the dragon's fiery breath.

The king Beowulf was fated to reach the end of his days together with his foe, the flaming serpent. Beowulf scorned the help of his warriors in this last fight. He did not fear the combat with the dragon. He had come through so many battles before—he had dared perilous waters, terrible clashes in war, he had cleansed Hrothgar's castle, and he had killed Grendel's evil mother.

Beowulf had fought with Hygelac against the Frisians, fought at the side of his lord until a sword stung Hygelac, drank his blood until he died. Then Beowulf had escaped the battle, broke through the shields of the enemy, and swum to freedom. While swimming he had saved 30 sets of armor from the Franks, river people who robbed the dead as they floated by. Forlorn and alone, Beowulf swam back a long distance to find his people. Hygd had offered him treasure and kingdom, rings and the throne. She did not trust her son, did not believe he could hold the throne against foreigners now that his father Hygelac was dead. Beowulf refused her offer. He would not rule while Hygelac's son was alive. Beowulf gave the son, Heardred, friendly wisdom. He gave all the help he could to help that young king rule well.

But Beowulf could not stop a group of exiled Swedes from coming to Geatland to seek protection. They were rebels against the king of Sweden, their famous uncle Onela. That hospitality caused the end of life for Heardred. Onela came after his nephews, the rebels, with a huge army. In the fight, Heardred died, wanting nothing more than to help his friends. Onela had no interest in the Geatish kingdom; he gave the throne to Beowulf.

As soon as he could, Beowulf aided Onela's nephew Eadgils, who was in exile. Beowulf sent him gold, an army, troops and weapons. He helped Eanmund win a bitter battle across the sea in Sweden. Eanmund won victory, and revenge, and the Swedish throne. Onela was slain.

Chapter 34

No matter what dangers Beowulf faced, no matter what battles, he survived them all. Then Beowulf met the dragon. Angered to his heart, the king of the Geats gathered twelve warriors and with them went to find the dragon. Beowulf knew by then what had caused the fiery destruction. Beowulf had in his possession that glorious cup; the slave had handed it to Beowulf. The slave was now the thirteenth of the company.

Wretched, afraid of both men and dragon, the slave had to do the warriors' bidding. The warriors asked the slave to take them to the dragon's lair. The slave took them to the hidden home of the dragon and showed them the huge stones that were set deep in the ground. The sea beat on the rocks nearby. Gems and gold were set in the walls of the dragon's ancient tower. Beowulf stared at the great tower, listening to the stories of the treasure heaped inside.

Inside his lair, the dragon waited, now awake and protecting those riches. It was ready to greet the great king, ready for combat. Taking that treasure would not be easy for any man.

Beowulf sat by the shore and rested. His soldiers gathered around him, wishing him well and urging him on. But Beowulf would not be cheered. His mind was heavy, restless, ripe for death. Fate was coming to the old man, and Beowulf could sense that. He was not fearful, but he felt that soon his spirit and his body would part, his blood spilled.

Then Beowulf spoke, retelling the tales of his success. "My early years were full of war. I survived every battle, and I still can remember each one. When I was seven years old, the king Hrethel took me from my father to raise me. He gave me jewels and feasts, raised me kindly and well. I was like a son to him, no less so than his own sons, Herebeald, Haethcyn, and Hygelac, who became my own king.

"Herebeald's life ended horribly. While he was hunting, Haethcyn, his brother, shot an arrow from his curved and horn-tipped bow. The arrow missed its mark and hit Herebeald, killing him. One son's blood was on the other son's arrow. There was no way to pay for this death, no way to avenge it. The deed was done, Haethcyn's guilt was great.

"Great also is the sorrow of an old man who watches his son swing from the gallows after scheming against the king. However aged, wise, and sad, the man can do nothing. Every morning he awakens and again remembers how his son died and again despairs. There will be no heir in the hall, and he does not want another. No future son matters. The wind sweeps through his son's empty dwelling. There is no sound of the harp, and there is no joy."

Chapter 35

Beowulf, the old king, continued. "Then, when the father crawls to his bed, the emptiness of the world and his home pierce him.

"So was it with Herebeald's father, the king. He could never settle scores, for the killer of one son was his other son. He did not hate Haethcyn, but he could no longer feel love for him. The sorrow was too great for him. He chose to die and go to God's light. As a good king does, he gave to his sons Haethcyn and Hygelac his land and riches when he died.

"Then, once again, war returned to the Swedes and the Geats. They had long hated each other. Once king Hrethel had died, the Swedes decided to attack. They did not want peace. At Hreosnabeorh they ambushed the Geats, slaughtering many.

"My fellow Geat warriors avenged that attack well. King Haethcyn paid with his life, which was a hard bargain. When dawn came the Swedes paid for that death—Hygelac slew the slayer. Hygelac's warriors got their revenge for the attack, death for death. A Geatish warrior attacked the Swedish king, Eofor, split his helmet and the skull beneath him, crashed the king to the ground in death.

"I earned the treasures and land Hygelac gave me, paid him in brave battles with my glittering sword. The king never needed to seek elsewhere for fighters, to give gold to better warriors of the Swedes or Danes. My sword was better, and it was always his. Always I walked before him; my place was in front. So it shall be forever, as long as my sword serves me.

"When I killed Daeghrefn, the champion of the Franks, it was with my bare hands. I crushed his bones, broke open his heart. Now, I will fight with both grip and sword."

Then Beowulf spoke his final boast. "I fought many battles when I was young. Now I am old, battle weary, but battle hard. If that grim burner of halls, that dragon, dares to come and meet me, I am ready."

Beowulf said farewell to his warriors, his dear companions, for the last time. "I would not bring sword or shield to this battle, if the dragon could be killed without it. I would rather crush it to death, grip the fire breather in my hands and tear it apart. But I expect hot flames, life-burning breath. Hot poison will leap from his tongue. So I feel no shame in dressing in mail shirt and armor.

"When the dragon comes to me, I will stand. Not one foot will I retreat. Here, by this wall, we will meet, and it must go between us as fate decides. My heart is firm, and I am ready. Wait in these woods, close by, my trusted warriors. We shall see which of us will manage to survive the vicious wounds of battle or fall here in death. No one else could help here; this is not your fight. Only I can meet this monster, do this hero's deed. I will succeed, win gold and the dragon's death by my courage, or the monster will bring me to a fiery death!"

Beowulf rose then, his iron shield and helmet shining. With his heart strong for battle, he walked to the tower, under the rocky cliffs. That was a deed no coward could have done.

Then, he who had triumphed in so many battles, stood so boldly, saw huge stone arches. Beneath them Beowulf could see the steam coming, the hot fire of the dragon's breath. The fire flowed down through the hidden entrance. It was too hot for mortals to stand. A spreading current of fire blocked the way. Beowulf's shield grew blistering hot. He could not enter without being burned by the dragon's flames.

The king of the Geats grew angry. He let a battle cry rise, roar out of his mouth. The cry was so loud and clear it reached the dragon, deep in his rock, and the dragon knew the anger of a hero. There was no more time to beg for peace.

From the cavern a roar of flame rolled out, and the earth shook. Outside the arches, Beowulf raised his shield in place against that strange terror. Scaly and coiled, the angry serpent was determined to have battle. Beowulf had already drawn his ancient sword. Its sharp edge gleamed.

The dragon came closer. The enemies were ready, each set on the destruction of the other and each fearful of the other. The Geats' great king stood firm, prepared for the battle. The dragon coiled, simmering with fury. Then it burst, roaring, toward Beowulf. Flames from the angry dragon licked at the iron shield. For a time the metal held, and the shield protected Beowulf, as he had planned. Then the shield began to melt, and for the first time in his life, Beowulf felt the fates were against him.

Beowulf lifted his treasure sword and struck the dragon's scaly hide. The ancient blade did bite into the dragon's skin and drew blood, but the blade failed the king. That ancient metal cracked on the dragon's bone, and it broke before it went deep enough to mortally wound the monster.

Mad with pain, the dragon grew more savage, spitting deadly fire. Beowulf did not boast then of his victories in battle. His treasured blade had failed him, the Geats' best weapon broken. This was no pleasant time for Beowulf, as he stared for the first time at death. This was a journey he was unwilling to make, that journey into darkness that all men must take.

Again, the enemies met. Seeing Beowulf's helplessness, the dragon came at him, sure it could end the battle. The dragon roared its fiery breath and Beowulf suffered, the flames encircling him. His companions, fearing for their lives, ran for the woods.

Only one of them remained there, his heart filled with sorrow. He remembered what loyalty meant.

Chapter 36

The loyal warrior's name was Wiglaf. He was the son of Weohstan; his family was once Swedish. He watched Beowulf suffer in agonizing flames, his helmet blistering with the heat. Wiglaf remembered everything his king Beowulf had given his family— armor and gold and great estates. Wiglaf could not stand idly by. He raised his shield and drew his sword, a treasured heirloom.

Weohstan had held the ancient sword for many winters, until his son was ready to be as brave as his graying father had been. When Weohstan died, his son inherited the sword, along with the gold and land. He had never worn the armor, or used the sword, until

Beowulf called him to fight against the dragon. With his companions gone, and Beowulf in agony, Wiglaf did not lose heart, nor did that ancient blade fail, as the dragon soon learned.

Wiglaf, with a heavy heart, spoke with scorn of his absent companions. "I remember when we sat in the castle drinking. We would boast of how brave we would be when Beowulf needed us. We said we would repay him his trust in us. We said we would repay him with our lives, if necessary, for the armor and treasures he had given us. He chose us for this battle—he thought we were worthy of fame! Beowulf meant to kill this dragon himself, as when he was younger and his strength amazed men.

"Now the day has come when Beowulf has need of help. In this battle, our king must rely on younger arms. We must help our lord, join him in this grim, fiery battle. I would rather be burned myself than to watch my king perish in the flames. Beowulf deserves better than this, to die alone, burned by this monster. I will stand alongside Beowulf, shield to shield, and aid him."

Wiglaf ran to Beowulf, spoke to his king. "Beloved Beowulf, do you remember you said you would never allow your good name to be tarnished? Now, you must be strong. My sword is here to aid you!"

The angry dragon heard these words, which made it more angry. The beast roared out its fiery answer to Wiglaf, anxious to finish off its hated foes. Fire from the dragon scorched Wiglaf's wooden shield, and it began to burn. The fierce flames seared through the shirts of mail. The young warrior jumped behind Beowulf's metal shield, still ready to help.

Beowulf gathered his strength, remembered his glorious name, and swung his sword, Naegling, against the dragon. The blade struck the dragon's neck bone and broke. The ancient sword Naegling had failed Beowulf—but no metal was ever a match for Beowulf's strength. His strength was too much. He could break the strongest blade.

For the third time that fearful fire dragon set upon the warriors again. Now wild with pain, it spewed fire, its fear forgotten in anger and agony. When the chance came, the grim fire monster sank its sharp fangs into Beowulf's neck. The king staggered with the deadly strike. His dark life blood flowed out in waves.

Chapter 37

Then Wiglaf showed himself a hero. When his king needed him most, Wiglaf was courageous. Paying no attention to the flames spewing from the dragon's mouth, Wiglaf came close, burning his hand to cinders as he did. Wiglaf ducked down and struck the dragon lower, buried his sword in the black belly of that serpent. The blade did its work well; the flames from the dragon began to slow.

The king, who was still able to move, managed to draw the battle-sharp knife he wore on his mail shirt. With a last burst of his old power, the king plunged his knife into that dragon's body, slashed its body in half. Together, Beowulf and Wiglaf had killed the beast, two noble warriors united in the dragon's death.

Alas, that moment of triumph was the last Beowulf would ever earn. The wound in his neck had begun to swell and burn. He could feel the dragon's poison burn in his veins, and he knew it was from the beast's deadly fangs. Beowulf stumbled slowly to the wall by the tower, lost in thought. Above him he saw huge stone arches. They were the work of giants and would be solid forever. Then Wiglaf's gentle hands bathed the wounds of his beloved king, fallen in battle. Carefully, Wiglaf unfastened Beowulf's helmet. He yearned to comfort his lord.

The mighty king spoke then, knowing he was soon to die from the dragon's evil bite. He could see that his days on earth had ended. All pleasure was gone, as his life would soon be gone. Beowulf said, "I would leave my armor to my son, had God granted me an heir. I have governed my people for 50 winters. In that time, there was no ruler in surrounding nations who dared to threaten me. My life has unwound as fate willed. I looked for no battles, was honest and patient. I was the best king I could be. Because of these things, I can leave this life contented.

"Now, quickly, Wiglaf, now that the body of the worm lies cooling, go to the dragon's lair and find the treasure. We have taken its life, and the gold is ours. Bring me the ancient silver, the shining jewels, the glittering armor and bright gems. I will more easily leave life and the kingdom so dear to me if I see this last treasure hoard."

Chapter 38

Wiglaf did as his dying king asked. He entered the dark cave with his mail shirt and his sword. The young warrior stepped through the vile smell of dragon breath and saw the treasure. There were piles of gleaming gold, precious jewels. In the dragon's lair were jeweled cups used long ago by men, now tarnished and broken, with no one to polish them. Littering the ground were old and rusty battle helmets, skillfully twisted bracelets. There was a golden battle flag, an intricate weaving of marvelous skill. From it shone a light that brightened the whole floor scattered with treasures. There was no more sign of the dragon, now dead.

Wiglaf took what he wanted, anything that pleased his eye. The young warrior loaded an armful of heavy plates and golden cups and that glorious banner. Wiglaf hurried back, anxious to show his lord the treasures before Beowulf died. He brought the treasure to Beowulf and found him bloody, gasping for breath, at the end of his life. Wiglaf once again bathed his king, soothed him until Beowulf could speak.

"For these fine trophies, this great treasure, I thank our Father in heaven," Beowulf said. "It is His grace that has allowed me to bring this gold hoard to my people. I gave my life for this treasure. Now it is your turn to lead, Wiglaf. Take this treasure and help my people. My time is over.

"After the funeral pyre, order a large burial mound to be made at the edge of the sea. Let the mound rise high. It is a memorial to my people. Ever after sailors shall call it 'Beowulf's Barrow.'[9] They will see it from the sea, and ships in the darkness will know it."

Then the brave dying king gave the golden necklace that was around his neck, symbol of his rule, to Wiglaf. He gave Wiglaf his rings, and his mail shirt. Beowulf ordered Wiglaf to use them well. "You are the last of our race. Fate has taken away our warriors in their strength and taken them to death. I must follow them." Those were the last words the brave king

---

9. barrow   a heap of rocks covering a grave

spoke. Soon, he would taste the hot flames of the funeral pyre. The soul left Beowulf's body and went to seek its place in heaven.

Chapter 39

Then Wiglaf was left to watch the last sufferings of the man he most loved on earth. His murderer also lay dead, the foul dragon cut in half, cold and still. Never again would that evil serpent guard the treasure he now lay near in death. No more would he thrash through the air at midnight, breathing poisonous flames, proud of his treasure hoard.

It is said, indeed, that there are no men, not even among the bravest of heroes, who would have dared to challenge the dragon, or even enter its lair. Beowulf had won that treasure only by his death—both man and dragon had ended their time.

When the battle was done, Beowulf's warriors crept out of the wood, ashamed, to where the fallen king and Wiglaf were. They waited for Wiglaf to speak. He was sitting near the body of Beowulf, desperately sprinkling water on the dead king, his heart heavy. Wiglaf could not, try though he would, keep any life in the old king, or stop the Lord's will.

Grimly, Wiglaf stared at the cowards, and then spoke angrily what men without courage must hear. "I say only the truth. The king gave you those fine ornaments, the swords and shields you bear. Then a battle came, and you ran like cowards when danger came. Yet God granted Beowulf the strength to help himself, swing his sword alone, win his own vengeance. I gave him the little help I could, gathering my courage to aid my king. I stabbed with my sword, and a weaker fire poured from the dragon's mouth. When Beowulf sorely needed help, too few of his warriors were here. Too few came when our king faced death.

"And now the giving of swords, of treasures and rich lands, is over. It is ended for you and everyone who shares your line. When other Geat warriors learn of your cowardice, you will go into the world in disgrace, your lands forfeited. Death is a better fate for any warrior than a life of shame!"

Chapter 40

Then Wiglaf commanded that the story of the battle be told to the Geats who waited anxiously for news, wondering if their king would return or be killed. The troop of warriors waiting hoped for the best. The messenger came to them.

"Now the lord of the Geats is on his death bed, killed by the dragon. But the dragon, too, is dead, cut in half by a knife blade. Not even Beowulf's strongest sword could pierce that dragon's head. Wiglaf sits in mourning, close by Beowulf's body. He is silent and sad, keeping watch over the king, in the place where both Beowulf and the dragon lie dead.

"We can expect an attack from the Franks and the Frisians, once they learn of Beowulf's death. The news will spread quickly. Hygelac began the feud with the Franks, raiding their villages along the Rhine River until they attacked him with a huge army and Hygelac was killed. Ever since, we have known no friendship with the Franks.

"Nor will there be peace with the Swedes. We all know how their old king, Ongentheow, took the life of our prince, Haethcyn, when in pride the Geats made war against the Swedes. That cunning old Swedish king let the Geatish warriors land on Swedish soil, and then he hit them with a lightning attack, taking treasure, rescuing the mother of Onela, and then killing Haethcyn. The Swedes chased the Geats to the wood. All that night the Swedes mocked the Geats, boasting they would finish them off at morning light. For sport, the Swedish king said he might hang a few Geats.

"With morning light came rescue—the sound of Hygelac's battle horns and the warriors who came with them. The sound turned downhearted Geats back into warriors."

Chapter 41

The messenger continued. "Then blood was everywhere, the warriors fighting fiercely. The Swedish king ordered his men back to the high ground, where there was a fortress to which they could escape. That king had heard of Hygelac, knew of his boldness and strength. He did not trust that his warriors could win. Hygelac's warriors did overrun that Swedish force, attacking the fortress.

"The Geats found the Swedish king, forcing him to face the Geats. One warrior, Wulf, swung his sword at the old king, smashing his helmet; blood poured from the wound. The Swedish king felt no fear. He returned a better blow than he received, savagely struck the Geatish warrior Wulf. The warrior staggered, tried to raise his sword, and then dropped it. The Swedish king had slashed through Wulf's helmet, and his head spouted blood. The cut was deep, but the Lord allowed the Geatish warrior Wulf to live and recover. But the Geat's brother Eofor, seeing the wound, set on the Swedish king, enraged. He swung his giant-made sword so hard the king's shield shattered and his life ended.

"When the Geats began to control the battle, many rushed forward to help bandage Wulf. Wulf's brother Eofor stripped the Swedish king of his armor and his sword, all his splendid war gear. He brought them all to Hygelac, his king. Hygelac thanked him and promised, there in front of all the warriors, that Eofor and Wulf would have wondrous gifts. He gave to each a hundred thousand units of land and gold. No watcher could be envious of those gifts—the feats it took to earn them were great. They had truly earned their glory in battle.

"These are all the feuds that still simmer. They will bring us to war with the Swedes as soon as they learn our lord Beowulf is dead and the Geats leaderless. We have lost the best of kings in Beowulf. He kept our enemies away, saved our land and our treasures for our people. He lived his whole life in bravery. Now let us hurry to the body of our king and bear him home and to his funeral pyre. With that dear heart shall melt that hoard from the dragon, bought with the blood of his own life. So shall flames eat all those grimly purchased riches. No warriors could wear shields bought so expensively, no maiden shall wear these gleaming necklaces on their necks."

So the messenger spoke to the people, a brave man with a truthful but sad message. The Geats rose. Sadly they walked down from the cliff, weeping as they saw the terrible sight. On the sand they found Beowulf, his life gone, their bold leader lying still in his final bed. He had reached the end of his mighty days, that great war lord.

The dragon was there too, the cold body of the fire snake stretched on the earth. It seethed no more with evil fire, but its scaly hide was grim and terrible, its many colors blackened by death. From end to end, the body was 50 feet long. This dragon had flown at night, in the silent darkness, back to his den. In death, he had returned once again. Beside him were heaped bracelets and cups crusted with gems, golden dishes, great ancient swords now eaten through with rust. It was as if they had all been in the earth for a thousand years.

In those days, that rich hoard was wrapped in a spell, so that no man might touch it or enter the tower until the Lord God, who watches over all, wished to let a man enter—that man and that man alone.

Chapter 42

The dragon that wrongly hid the treasure there had no happiness in those riches, nor any profit. It killed Beowulf while jealously guarding that glittering hoard, but then the dragon was punished for that with death. No one knows when princes and warriors, all the bravest and strongest of men, are destined to die. No one knows when his time will end, his halls empty. So it was with Beowulf, who fought the dragon but could not know that death would come to him.

The spell on that treasure was set by men now long dead. Those men laid on the hoard a spell so deep that the man who troubled the treasure would be cursed until the end of the world. The unlucky man who stole their treasure out of greed would be punished with misery—kept fast in bonds of hell and tortured. God alone could break the magic of that spell, open the hoard to one the Lord favored.

Then Wiglaf spoke. "It often happens that an entire country will suffer because of the will of one man. That has happened to us. We could not persuade our dear king not to attack the dragon. We urged Beowulf to leave the deadly serpent in the dark, to let him brood until the end of the world. Beowulf's will was too strong. Now the hoard has been bought with his life, but our king was worth much more than this treasure.

"When Beowulf was dying, he asked me to gather the riches to show him. I gathered a huge armful of treasure, bright gold and gemstones, and carried it outside for my king to see. He was lying right there, still alive. In sorrow, he spoke. These were his commands. He said I should greet you all. He asked that after his body was burned, you bring his ashes here, and on this spot on the shore make a high barrow, as great and lasting as his fame. At that place would his people remember him, remember that he was the most worthy king who lived.

"Come, let me show you the hoard of treasure inside these walls. We should see the dragon's marvel one more time. I shall lead you, so you can see the gold and the rings, and the jewels. Prepare the bier[10] while we gaze at the treasure. When we come out, we will

10. **bier** a platform on which a dead body or coffin is placed

carry our beloved Beowulf to where he will lie forever in the Lord's keeping."

Wiglaf the brave announced that all the warriors, everyone who owned a dwelling, come from near and far with lumber to place on the king's pyre.

"The fire must gnaw at his body, rise with black flames roaring," Wiglaf said. "Our dear king has endured arrows in showers, weapons barbed and sharp. Now he will endure the flames."

Wiglaf chose seven of the most noble Geats and led them deep into the dragon's lair, beneath the evil roof. The warrior in front held a torch high. So vast was the treasure, with gold and jewels all over the ground, that the Geats did not bother to draw lots to see who would get it. There was so much. The eight carried as much of the treasure out as they could. Then they pushed the dragon over the wall, down the cliff, and let the ocean take that evil worm. The warriors loaded the treasure on a cart—incredible wealth—with the body of their dear king Beowulf. They brought it all across the sand to the cliff where the funeral pyre awaited.

Chapter 43

The Geats had made ready an enormous funeral pyre. Hung around it were helmets, and battle shields, and gleaming mail shirts. All was as Beowulf had asked. The bearers brought the body of their beloved king and lay the body high on the wood. All were weeping.

Then the great fire was begun. The smoke from the wood climbed high, black above the flames. The roaring fire danced and crackled, while all around were the moans and cries of Beowulf's sorrowful people. The fire burned until it had consumed Beowulf's bone house, burned to the heart. Sad in spirit, the Geats cried for their lost king.

In the same way did one Geatish woman, her hair bound up, sing a song of grief for Beowulf. Over and over she sang her song of misery, of endless sadness. She sang of her fears that raiders would attack, that there would be many slaughters, and Geatish warriors in terror. Heaven swallowed the smoke.

Then the Geats built the tower as Beowulf had asked. It was strong and tall, a tower that sailors could easily see from the sea. In ten days they had completed this monument to Beowulf. The ashes, the remains of the pyre, were buried in the walls. The riches Beowulf and Wiglaf had won at such a high price from the dragon—the rings, the necklaces, the ancient, well-wrought armor—were all left there too. The gold and silver were returned to the stony ground, back to the earth. They were forever hidden, and forever useless to men. The earth now owned these riches. It owns them still.

The bravest Geats rode their horses around the barrow, 12 of them. They wanted to mourn their king. They told stories of Beowulf and his greatness, his glory. They praised him for his heroic deeds. They spoke of a life as noble as any on this earth. They cried that no better king had ever lived, that no king was more generous to his warriors, or more courageous. Beowulf was the kindest of kings, they said, and the most deserving of fame.

REVIEWING YOUR READING

PROLOGUE–CHAPTER 7

FINDING THE MAIN IDEA

1. In Chapter 3, the author is mainly telling about

    (A) the early history of the Danish kings. (B) how Grendel had savaged the castle of Hrothgar. (C) how the Danes had tried to fight Grendel. (D) the journey of Beowulf and his warriors to Denmark.

REMEMBERING DETAILS

2. Beowulf has traveled to fight Grendel because

    (A) he has done similar things before and thinks he will win in a fight against the monster. (B) Beowulf has a spell of strength on him that makes him always successful in battle. (C) his king, Hygelac, has forced him to come. (D) he wants to be king, and fighting Grendel is the best way to make this happen.

DRAWING CONCLUSIONS

3. The castle Heorot is empty at night because

    (A) most of the warriors have been killed. (B) no warrior dares to sleep there with Grendel on the loose. (C) Hrothgar has forbidden his warriors to sleep there. (D) both A and B.

IDENTIFYING THE MOOD

4. The mood of Beowulf when he comes to the castle to meet the king is best described as

    (A) proud. (B) timid. (C) kind. (D) angry.

CRITICAL THINKING

5. **Knowledge** Describe what has happened in Denmark to bring Beowulf there.

6. **Comprehension** Explain why Beowulf feels he can win in a battle with Grendel when none of the Danish warriors have been able to kill the monster.

7. **Comprehension** Why does Grendel attack the castle and the warriors there?

CHAPTERS 8–14

FINDING THE MAIN IDEA

1. Chapters 11 and 12 are mainly about

    (A) Unferth's conflict with Beowulf. (B) the return of the Danish warriors to the castle. (C) the battle between Grendel and Beowulf. (D) how Beowulf's warriors defeated Grendel.

REMEMBERING DETAILS

2. Beowulf was able to beat Grendel because of
    (A) his strong grip. (B) the support of his warriors. (C) the prayers of Hrothgar. (D) his enormous sword, Hrunting.

DRAWING CONCLUSIONS

3. You can conclude that one reason Grendel had not been defeated before was

    (A) the monster had laid spells that blunted warriors' weapons. (B) the Danes were not brave enough. (C) the Danes were afraid to fight Grendel. (D) Hrothgar had forbidden his warriors to fight Grendel.

IDENTIFYING THE MOOD

4. When Hrothgar leaves the castle and allows Beowulf and his men to sleep there, Hrothgar's mood could best be described as

    (A) defeated. (B) hopeful. (C) skeptical. (D) regretful.

CRITICAL THINKING

5. **Analysis** Contrast the tale of Breca and Beowulf as told by Unferth and by Beowulf.

6. **Comprehension** Why does Beowulf do nothing as he watches Grendel rip apart one of the Geat warriors?

7. **Knowledge** Describe the battle between Grendel and Beowulf.

CHAPTERS 15–21

FINDING THE MAIN IDEA

1. Chapter 19 is mostly about

   (A) the death of Hnaef. (B) Hrothgar's rewards to Beowulf after he kills Grendel. (C) how the Danes return to the castle and clean it after Grendel is killed. (D) how the celebration after Grendel's death turns to misery after Grendel's mother strikes.

REMEMBERING DETAILS

2. Grendel's mother takes revenge for her son's death by

   (A) kidnapping Beowulf. (B) murdering another warrior. (C) ripping apart the castle. (D) warning that she will continue her son's work.

DRAWING CONCLUSIONS

3. When Unferth gave Beowulf his sword so Beowulf could use it against Grendel's mother, that meant

   (A) Unferth now trusted Beowulf. (B) Unferth had given up his honor by giving Beowulf the sword. (C) Unferth was pledging his loyalty to Beowulf. (D) Unferth wanted Beowulf to fail.

IDENTIFYING THE MOOD

4. When Hrothgar tells Beowulf of Grendel's mother's attack, his mood could best be described as one of

   (A) despair. (B) indifference. (C) satisfaction. (D) disgust.

CRITICAL THINKING

5. **Knowledge** Identify reasons why Hengest broke the peace between the Danes and Frisians by killing Finn.

6. **Comprehension** Explain why the attack by Grendel's mother is particularly hard for King Hrothgar.

7. **Comprehension** Why do you think Hrothgar's description of the lake where Grendel's mother lives is so gruesome? What is he hoping to accomplish with this description?

CHAPTERS 22–26

FINDING THE MAIN IDEA

1. In Chapters 22–23, the main thing that happens is

    (A) Beowulf returns home to the Geats. (B) Beowulf battles Grendel's mother in the lake. (C) Grendel's mother lures Beowulf to her home at the bottom of the lake. (D) Hrothgar rewards Beowulf for killing Grendel's mother.

REMEMBERING DETAILS

2. Beowulf finally kills Grendel's mother

    (A) with his bare hands. (B) with Hrunting, Unferth's sword. (C) with a giant's sword he finds in the cave. (D) with the giant's sword he brings with him.

DRAWING CONCLUSIONS

3. Beowulf chops off Grendel's head and brings it back to the castle because

    (A) he promised he would bring it to Wealhtheow. (B) he knew Hrothgar needed it to break a spell. (C) it is a final act of vengeance against Grendel. (D) unless the monster's head is chopped off, the monster may be able to live again and murder the Danes.

IDENTIFYING THE MOOD

4. When the Danish warriors see the blood rising from the lake, their mood is

    (A) one of victory: Beowulf has triumphed. (B) one of panic: Beowulf is in trouble. (C) one of grief: Beowulf is dead. (D) one of indifference: Beowulf has died at the monster's hand just like all the rest of the warriors.

CRITICAL THINKING

5. **Comprehension** Explain why the giant's sword melted after Beowulf used it to kill Grendel's mother.

6. **Comprehension** Why does Hrothgar tell Beowulf the story of Heremond?

7. **Analysis** Which of Beowulf's battles do you think was harder, the battle with Grendel or the battle with Grendel's mother? Support your argument with details from the story.

CHAPTERS 27–32

FINDING THE MAIN IDEA

1. The main point of chapters 28–30 is

   (A) for Beowulf to explain to Hygelac what happened in Denmark. (B) that the dragon awakens. (C) that Beowulf becomes king of the Geats. (D) that Beowulf becomes king of Denmark.

REMEMBERING DETAILS

2. As a child, Beowulf was
   (A) known for his courage. (B) extraordinarily strong.
   (C) left to fend for himself. (D) thought worthless.

DRAWING CONCLUSIONS

3. You can conclude that the author wants the slave who steals the dragon's cup to be seen as

   (A) someone who steals whenever he can. (B) a careless person.
   (C) someone who has unknowingly caused the dragon to stir.
   (D) someone who will do anything for his master and does not care what the result is for anyone else.

IDENTIFYING THE MOOD

4. The mood of the dragon when it discovers the cup is gone could best be described as

   (A) unhappy. (B) resigned. (C) sorrowful. (D) enraged.

CRITICAL THINKING

5. **Knowledge** Describe the relationship of Hygelac and Beowulf in the years after Beowulf returned from slaying Grendel and his mother.

6. **Analysis** Compare and contrast the dragon and Grendel.

7. **Synthesis** Write a short description of Beowulf's life up to this point.

CHAPTERS 33–37

FINDING THE MAIN IDEA

1. The most important event that happens in Chapters 35–36 is that

    (A) Beowulf rules his people well for many years. (B) Beowulf fights the dragon. (C) a dragon lays waste to the Geats' land. (D) Beowulf tells stories about the history of his people.

REMEMBERING DETAILS

2. Heardred is killed by

    (A) his brother. (B) his father. (C) Beowulf. (D) the Swedes.

DRAWING CONCLUSIONS

3. When the author tells the reader, "But Beowulf would not be cheered. His mind was heavy, restless, ripe for death," as Beowulf prepares to fight the dragon, the reader knows

    (A) Beowulf will survive this battle, too. (B) that Beowulf will not survive this battle. (C) that Beowulf is still the strongest man in the world. (D) that Beowulf's warriors have no fear that he will lose.

IDENTIFYING THE MOOD

4. When Wiglaf realizes he is the only warrior who has not deserted Beowulf, Wiglaf's mood is

    (A) of even greater courage. (B) one of scorn for the absent warriors. (C) fearful. (D) reflective.

CRITICAL THINKING

5. **Knowledge** Describe the results of the dragon's anger on Beowulf's kingdom.

6. **Comprehension** Explain why Herebeald's father died of grief.

7. **Analysis** Compare and contrast Beowulf as he fought Grendel and Grendel's mother and Beowulf as he fought the dragon.

CHAPTERS 38–43

FINDING THE MAIN IDEA

1.   The main idea of Chapters 40–41 is

(A) a description of what probably lies ahead for the Geats, and a description of the funeral for Beowulf. (B) a description of how Beowulf died and who will now rule the country. (C) an accounting of what happened to the warriors who ran away. (D) a description of how terrible life is after Beowulf dies.

REMEMBERING DETAILS

2.   The treasure from the dragon's lair

(A) is returned to the lair. (B) is placed with Beowulf's funeral pyre. (C) is given to Wiglaf for his courage. (D) is distributed to all the Geats.

DRAWING CONCLUSIONS

3.   You can conclude that the warriors who did not help Beowulf

(A) will be exiled. (B) will become Wiglaf's trusted warriors. (C) will be rewarded by Beowulf's enemies. (D) will all be killed by the Danes in vengeance.

IDENTIFYING THE MOOD

4.   At the funeral, the mood of the Geats is one of

(A) accusation. (B) sorrow. (C) anger. (D) relief.

CRITICAL THINKING

5.   **Comprehension** How do you know Wiglaf will be the next king of the Geats?

6.   **Application** Why do you think the messenger prophesies feuds and battles after Beowulf's death?

7.   **Evaluation** Wiglaf says, "It often happens that an entire country will suffer because of the will of one man." What does Wiglaf mean, and why does he say this?